LEARNING IN THE PLURAL

TRANSFORMATIONS IN HIGHER EDUCATION:
THE SCHOLARSHIP OF ENGAGEMENT

LEARNING IN THE PLURAL

Essays on the Humanities

and Public Life

David D. Cooper
Foreword by Julie Ellison
Afterword by Scott J. Peters
and Timothy K. Eatman

Michigan State University Press
East Lansing

♾ The paper used in this publication meets the minimum requirements of ANSI/NISO
Z39.48-1992 (R 1997) (Permanence of Paper).

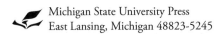 Michigan State University Press
East Lansing, Michigan 48823-5245

Printed and bound in the United States of America.

20 19 18 17 16 15 14 1 2 3 4 5 6 7 8 9 10

LIBRARY OF CONGRESS CATALOGING-IN-PUBLICATION DATA

Cooper, David D.
    Learning in the plural : essays on the humanities and public life / David D. Cooper;
foreword by Julie Ellison; afterword by Scott J. Peters and Timothy K. Eatman.
        pages cm.
    Includes bibliographical references.
    ISBN 978-1-61186-112-9 (cloth : alk. paper)—ISBN 978-1-60917-402-6 (ebook) 1.
Humanities—Philosophy. 2. City and town life. I. Title.

AZ103.C59 2014
001.301—dc23   2013020463

Book design by Scribe Inc. (www.scribenet.com)
Cover design by Shaun Allshouse, www.shaunallshouse.com
Cover image ©David D. Cooper and is used with permission

g green
  press
  INITIATIVE Michigan State University Press is a member of the Green Press Initiative and
is committed to developing and encouraging ecologically responsible publishing
practices. For more information about the Green Press Initiative and the use of recycled
paper in book publishing, please visit www.greenpressinitiative.org.

Visit Michigan State University Press at www.msupress.org

TRANSFORMATIONS IN HIGHER EDUCATION: SCHOLARSHIP OF ENGAGEMENT

THE TRANSFORMATIONS IN HIGHER EDUCATION: SCHOLARSHIP OF Engagement book series is designed to provide a forum where scholars can address the diverse issues provoked by community-campus partnerships that are directed toward creating innovative solutions to societal problems. Numerous social critics and key national commissions have drawn attention to the pervasive and burgeoning problems of individuals, families, communities, economies, health services, and education in American society. Such issues as child and youth development, economic competitiveness, environmental quality, and health and health care require creative research and the design, deployment, and evaluation of innovative public policies and intervention programs. Similar problems and initiatives have been articulated in many other countries, apart from the devastating consequences of poverty that burdens economic and social change. As a consequence, there has been increasing societal pressure on universities to partner with communities to design and deliver knowledge applications that address these issues, and to co-create novel approaches to effect system changes that can lead to sustainable and evidence-based solutions. Knowledge generation and knowledge application are critical parts of the engagement process, but so too are knowledge dissemination and preservation. The *Transformations in Higher Education: Scholarship of Engagement* series was designed to meet one aspect of the dissemination/preservation dyad.

This series is sponsored by the National Collaborative for the Study of University Engagement (NCSUE) and is published in partnership with the Michigan State University Press. An external board of editors supports the NCSUE editorial staff in order to insure that all volumes in the series are peer reviewed throughout the publication process. Manuscripts embracing campus-community partnerships are invited from authors regardless of discipline, geographic place, or type of transformational change accomplished. Similarly, the series embraces all methodological approaches from rigorous randomized trials to narrative and ethnographic studies. Analyses may span the qualitative to quantitative continuum, with particular emphasis on mixed-model approaches. However, all manuscripts must attend to detailing critical aspects of partnership development, community involvement, and evidence of program changes or impacts. Monographs and books provide ample space for authors to address all facets of engaged scholarship thereby building a compendium of praxis that will facilitate replication and generalization, two of the cornerstones of evidence-based programs, practices, and policies. We invite you to submit your work for publication review and to fully participate in our effort to assist higher education to renew its covenant with society through engaged scholarship.

Hiram E. Fitzgerald
Burton Bargerstock
Laurie Van Egeren

For Christina,
Again and Always

CONTENTS

FOREWORD: ON THE BUS

JULIE ELLISON

THE TRUE BEGINNING OF *LEARNING IN THE PLURAL* COMES IN THE middle of the book, in the 2002 essay, "Bus Rides and Forks in the Road: The Making of a Public Scholar." As a chronically nonsequential reader, I am only half joking when I propose that the reader of this book start here—especially if that reader cares about college teachers. You will accompany David Cooper as he recalls his three-stop bus route through Providence, Rhode Island, in the early 1970s: "Facing unemployment lines jammed with fellow baby boomer academics and without the slightest prospect for a full-time tenure track position, I managed nonetheless to cobble together three part-time teaching jobs."

Improvised employment caused him "to experience, during a single semester . . . the full institutional spectrum of American postsecondary education," inseparable from the social architecture and built environments of urban neighborhoods, in which religious as well as economic history is embedded.

> After covering a couple sections of freshman English at Rhode Island College, I walked a few blocks through a working-class neighborhood in

North Providence and caught the in-bound Smith Street bus. I hopped off a few stops later at Providence College, where I taught another Composition course. Back on the bus, I transferred downtown to an East Side bus that groaned up the Benefit Street tunnel past the magisterial Unitarian Church and by blue-blood mansions. The bus dropped me off in front of Brown University's Rockefeller Library, where I presided over a senior seminar in Religious Studies.

Were any of us tempted to look back nostalgically on the seventies as a time when it was easier to come of age, to educate, to be educated, or to gain institutional sanction for democratic pedagogies, *Learning in the Plural* will helpfully disabuse us of that sentiment. Cooper also speaks powerfully to stresses and inequities that persist today. He provides us with important questions to ask as we undertake our own inquiries into how we do civic engagement in the era when contract faculty are the "new faculty majority."

His narrative creates a space for a multigenerational investigation—an inquiry at once visceral and cerebral—of structural change in higher education in landscapes of contingency. For Cooper, the career-long tour of educational geographies, propelled by an "insanely competitive job market," takes him to Providence, then California (as a "decade-long houseguest in English"), and finally to East Lansing for a temporary instructorship that became a tenured position with its own constraints.

The story of the bus ride becomes central to the book as a report on the unnerving conditions of the faculty "houseguest," visitor, "temporary" or uneasy colleague. One important lesson of this chapter is that we should pay attention to the geographies and temporalities—places and times—of educational work. *Learning in the Plural* values individual character. It also values the character of places, institutions, and systems, and explores "alienation" and "dislocation" as dimensions of professional citizenship. Providence, California, mid-Michigan: these are all stops on Cooper's career-long journey. The bus, for Cooper, is always a school bus—indeed, it is always school.

A close reading of the bus ride that took Cooper to contingent-faculty gigs at three campuses in Providence includes a sustained encounter with the feelings and thoughts that this memory arouses. The complex affects in this section of the book, while historically grounded in a different time, are strongly felt in the present, as well. The story of the bus ride requires us to pay attention to what Kathleen Woodward calls "intellectual morale."

At the time, Cooper "dimly imagined the bus ride as a symbolic journey along an institutional axis that defined the organizing polarities of higher learning in America." And indeed, a metaphoric reading is irresistible. Cooper's bus ride as allegory works better than ever at what David Scobey calls our "Copernican revolution" in American and global higher education. He is looking out the window at campuses where some faculty are in place, not displaced. He is also looking at the places between campuses and between bus stops: the kind of neighborhoods that, decades later, he will enter through new relationships organized around writing and the teaching of writing.

Allegories, like fairy tales and parables, typically work in sets of three, and this one is true to type. It is artfully told: three socioeconomically distinct neighborhoods; three colleges in ascending order of status and geographical elevation; three courses, composition for freshman and a seminar for seniors. The craft of Cooper's vignette cannot disguise the fact that this bus ride was the consequence of jarring disconnects of space, time, and persona—the material realities of being a contingent faculty member before the term was common. Yet at the same time, the bus ride shows how we can "learn in the plural" through isolated experiences that are nonetheless systemically connected—"plural."

The multiple-personality sensation of holding "cobbled together" part-time jobs, familiar to so many contract faculty members today, is countered only by the reflective consciousness of the bus-riding instructor—who became the narrator—as he "tacks" between "the extremes and contradictions" of an "open-admission state college" (a "College of Opportunity" for first-generation college students), Providence College, a Catholic institution with a strong Dominican tradition; and Brown University, a "highly selective, richly endowed private university." Even at the time, he recalls mining the bus ride for its meanings, seeking "a personal myth that would make some sense out of the fear, second-guessing, and inner turbulence I was feeling at the precarious threshold of a career."

The "work" of these "working neighborhoods" includes the work of the campuses located in and near them. In the mid-eighties, the national office of Campus Compact moved to Providence. The nineties saw a remapping of downtown Providence through the I-way project, which uncovered built-over rivers and rerouted streets. The 2000s saw the founding of the Feinstein Institute for Public Service under the leadership of Rick Battistoni at Providence College and Brown University's Slavery and Justice Project, an examination into campus and city initiated by President Ruth Simmons and led by historian James Campbell. As in virtually every city in the United States, the civic engagement movement in higher education, to which Cooper has made such a rich contribution, would take powerful hold in the landscape of that early "turbulence."

Later in "Bus Rides and Forks in the Road," early-career stress yields to a midlife crisis in "a career marked"—up to its civic turning point—by "conflict, separation, division, suspicion, and isolation." Institutional misery yields a hard-won turn to civic collegiality, an organizational phenomenon that registers as "a pull of intimacy and belonging toward my new university." The positive role played by institutions "in shaping my identity and integrity became more important and obvious." Many publicly engaged scholars—myself included—report a similar growth spurt in organizational thinking. Indeed, I have come to think of this trend as opening the way to a new area of the public humanities that we might call cultural organizational studies. Cooper's contribution here lies in his attention to both the conceptual and the emotional dimensions of organizational life. After "retooling as a public scholar" (15), he sees more clearly both the systemic nature of institutional alienation and its flip side—the way in which institutions can be "sources of affirmation, acceptance, and individuation," especially when they support collegial forms of civic engagement. A major consequence of Cooper's "civic turn" is this appreciation of institutional positivity as it affects his "teaching life." He testifies to the "pull of intimacy and belonging toward my new university" accompanied by an analysis of the integrative "role that institutions play": "I became compelled to see the world around me and my place in it as a complex network of connections, integrations, balances, couplings, and ties that bind, and not a place of chaos, division, irreconcilable differences, and movement against the grain."

Cooper's defines the humanities as a way of life. The bus ride, Cooper recalls, "was a practical education in what the humanities were all about: commitment to the social witness of ideas, intellectual community, and the arc of hope that scribes the moral lives of students." Note how Cooper uses "scribes" as a verb here. This is not accidental. Writing was his "vehicle" for engagement. We should attend closely to the details of Cooper's story of how he worked his way toward a new professional identity, combining skills as "an editor, teacher, and writer," practices such as writing "nontechnical prose accessible to the world outside the academy," and a community of practice that possessed a "model"— service-learning pedagogy. It was a change in his writing practice that took him from the readerly position of the young academic looking at Providence from the bus windows or the scholar of Thomas Merton to finding "a wealth of new opportunities." First as "editorial consultant" to the Center for Urban Affairs, and later as a teacher of general-education writing courses, he found, in sociable writing, with community partners, a new kind of mobility and connection.

Cooper's hard-earned public humanism sends a message to reflective civic practitioners everywhere: public engagement needs humanists' ability to think narratively, emotionally, historically, ethically—and organizationally. For him, the humanities are most salient when they "bridge private lives and public obligations," serving as "a means of inviting citizens to be interpreters of their own lives while bringing critical resources . . . to bear on social and cultural renewal." But Cooper, caught between "the quest for self-purpose" and "the standards by which the profession regards [him]," is cranky about the humanities, too. "The profession" (by which he means something like Thomas Bender's "disciplinary professionalism") and poststructuralist theory together form Cooper's Scylla and Charybdis. Cooper comes to "the national service-learning movement and the practice of public scholarship" through his critique of the faculty rewards system and his exasperation with "the contemporary humanities," with which he was long "at odds." Cooper felt that his "passion for convergence" resisted a "new generation of academics." He was irritated by postmodernist "skepticism" and was fundamentally at odds with the emphasis on "difference" rather than "common knowledge and common truths" (11). He recalls seeking to "transcend difference and seek common ground with others," viewing his "humanities colleagues" as "abstract, contentious, and theory-driven" characters who were opting out of "integration."

This marks a clash of generational cultures. Though I am only a little younger than Cooper, beginning my teaching career in 1980, I am part of that once-new generation. I have held on to some elements of that "agenda" and loosened my grip on others, but without rancor. A few years before Cooper wrote this essay, I was going through my own version of the "civic turn," and on my bus ride, plenty of Cooper's antagonists were my allies. In my view, it is precisely critical reframing linked to important social and cultural movements that led to some of the richest environments for public scholarship we have. I have my own version of professional integration, a story that connects community cultural development with the local and global commitments of ethnic studies, postcolonial studies, women's and gender studies, and whiteness studies, and studies of literacy, along with a flow of new methodologies into the humanities: ethnography, performance, exhibition, documentary, PhotoVoice, life writing. These developments—embodied in the work of Tiya Miles, John Kuo Wei Tchen, Robin Bachin, the authors of *Latina Testimonios*, George Sanchez, Diana Taylor, and Gregory Jay—transpose several generative areas of critical theory into public scholarship without resentment.

Cooper thus sets himself apart from "younger colleagues." But today's students and faculty also owe a debt of gratitude to David Cooper as an educational quester, a debt that can be repaid by a careful reading of his reflections on the stations of a career. He shares common ground with such astute readers of the humanities in American universities as Christopher Newfield, whose book *The Unmaking of the Middle Class*, includes a compelling analysis of theoretical choices that either enabled or blocked the exercise of "institutional agency" by humanities faculty. Despite his occasional testiness, then, Cooper invites a robust cross-generational dialogue with today's publicly engaged humanists in the early stages of their careers. They, too, face "a moribund job market," possess "a nascent feeling for a dynamic and integrative learning life," and are trying to translate that intuition, or tacit knowledge, into civic and institutional agency. The chances of college teachers enjoying a "bus ride with tenure" are slimmer, but at the same time contract faculty, because they are more numerous, are better organized to think critically about the lives of humanities scholars, through, for example, alt-ac, the New Faculty Majority, and The Adjunct Project 2.0. In universities, as in schools, municipal offices, manufacturing plants, newspaper offices, and dozens of other settings, work identities are being second-guessed, revised, renegotiated—or lost. Cooper's "Bus Rides and Forks in the Road"—along with the rest of this fine book—speak to how we live now, which is less different from how we lived then than we might wish. Precisely because Cooper tells a story of stressful improvisation in the context of systemic change, he offers us a model narrative of the scholar as an always-in-process civic professional.

INTRODUCTION

THE TEN ESSAYS IN *LEARNING IN THE PLURAL* ARE SELECTED FROM
dozens of articles, chapters, reviews, and commentaries I have published during the past two decades on the humanities, literacy, and public life. They
address important issues head on and raise often-provocative questions about
the relevance and roles of humanities teaching and scholarship, the moral
footings and public purposes of the humanities, engaged teaching practices,
institutional and disciplinary reform, academic professionalism, and public
scholarship in a democracy. Those questions boil down to core queries that
have sustained, prodded, and vexed my career: Can civic engagement rescue
the humanities from a prolonged identity crisis? How can the practices and
methods, the conventions and innovations of humanities teaching and scholarship yield knowledge that contributes to the public good?

Unlike most public humanities practitioners, I view public work in
the humanities as a corrective to and a critique of prevailing critical practices that have taken hold in the academy during the past thirty years
and cut off the cultural disciplines from meaningful participation in
democratic renewal, education for citizenship, and public problem solving. These essays are designed, then, to stir discussion about the purposes
of the humanities and the problems we face during an era of declining
institutional support, public alienation and misunderstanding, student

ambivalence, and diminishing resources. The questions I raise in this book
are uncomfortable and, in my view, necessary for reflection, renewal, and
reform. They include frank, critical assessments of intellectual trends that
shadowed my career as a public-minded teacher/scholar and continue to
prevail in the humanities, including postmodernism, multiculturalism,
identity politics, and the hard turn from the pragmatic moral questions of
liberal humanism to the ultraspecialized languages of cultural and postcolonial studies, hybrid subfields, critical pedagogy, and high theory. I
address social currents—for example, intergenerational conflict, education reform debates, academic meritocracy, stress on the tenure system,
the land-grant tradition, and the institutional citizenship and civic
engagement movements—that sometimes ran counter to those trends,
sometimes added to their momentum. I probe the moral, ethical, social,
philosophical, and theoretical foundations of the teaching and learning
enterprise as I practiced it and as I witnessed the way it was practiced
around me. I also report on active learning initiatives that reenergized my
own teaching life while reshaping the teaching mission of the humanities,
including service learning, collaborative learning, the learning community
movement, and student-centered and deliberative pedagogy.

From early efforts to articulate core concepts like social idealism, civic
virtue, and moral literacy to a mid-career meditation on liberal education
climate change and a recent report on the power of deliberative democracy as
a teaching and learning resource, these ten essays, organized chronologically,
scribe an arc across the career of a teaching humanist devoted to learning in
community and community in learning—to "learning in the plural." The
arc is hardly an even or uninterrupted line of accumulated knowledge or
wisdom. In fact, it may more closely resemble an EKG, a rhythm of returns
to the same, or related, issues and queries scrolled out across twenty years.
In short, not a smooth trajectory but a bumpy ride.

Many of these articles and essays are excursions in active and improvisa-
tional thinking in which the questions I raise and the uncertainties I probe are
more important than answers arrived at or ground defended. Moreover, in an
effort to gain my bearings and set my compass points, I often move against the
grain and away from prevailing critical fashion or received opinion.

In the lead essay on civic literacy and social idealism, for example, I explore a moral self-enclosure I see among my students that leaves them indifferent to the obsessions over "difference" and "the other" that dominated—and continue to dominate—humanities curricula, pedagogy, theory, and scholarship in the early 1990s. In the next essay, "Moral Literacy," I turn to examine in more scholarly fashion the moral dimensions of language competency at a time—1994—when the very term "moral" was completely anathema and retrograde to literacy theorists and culture critics. Partly in response to these pedagogical and critical trends, in the next essay, "Reading, Writing, and Reflection," I take a more pragmatic, grounded, inside look at my early efforts to infuse active learning techniques into my own humanities classes.

"The Changing Seasons of Liberal Learning," the fourth essay, takes on a nasty, reactionary undercurrent of student animus that surfaced briefly in the late 1990s. In that essay I explore the political and social changes that had swept over college campuses since the 1960s. In addition to calling out the so-called Millennial Generation, I turn the critical spotlight onto my own generation, the boomer juggernaut that swelled faculty ranks by the turn of the present century.

In the fifth essay, "Academic Professionalism and the Betrayal of the Land-Grant Tradition," I take a largely dim and disappointing look at an important historical force in American higher education that has both kindled within me a passionate feel for democracy and challenged me as a teacher/scholar with broken promises, especially about the humanities' role in protecting the university's part of the social contract against the encroachments of status professionalism, overspecialization, theoretical mumbo jumbo, and heightened competitiveness that prevailed in the academic humanities by the year 2000—an ethos the philosopher Richard Rorty described as "a Gothic world in which democratic politics has become a farce."

I consider the sixth essay, "Bus Rides and Forks in the Road: The Making of a Public Scholar," a risky but pivotal contribution. It is an unvarnished autobiographical reflection on the forces and the frictions that shaped me as a public teacher/scholar. I expose some raw vulnerabilities in an effort, as I say, "to reconcile the quest for self-purpose, aspiration, commitment, and self-respect—the larger rhythms, in other words, of an individual moral life—against those standards by which the profession regards me and, by extension, trains me to regard myself."

The next three essays zero in on specific pathways of a larger systematic journey I undertook during the next decade to incorporate civic engagement into my classes and to practice public humanities scholarship and the scholarship of teaching: "Education for Democracy: A Conversation in Two Keys," "Is Civic Discourse Still Alive?," and "Four Seasons of Deliberative Learning." As I note specifically about the latter essay, all these pieces describe some of the engaged learning techniques I tried out along the way. They are also lab reports on the experiments I conducted. And they are partly travelogues about the highs and lows of the trip—the exhilarating discoveries I made, the company I kept, as well as the wrong turns I took and jams I got into.

The closing essay—"Can Civic Engagement Rescue the Humanities?"—is a polemic that will win me few friends. The answers I give—"a reluctant no. And a qualified yes."—are intended to challenge future humanities scholar/teachers to remember their public obligations.

BELIEVING IN DIFFERENCE: THE ETHICS OF CIVIC LITERACY (1993)

I CAN THINK OF NO MORE URGENT MOMENT THAN NOW FOR UNDER-graduate educators to be asking ethical questions about the content and context of a liberal arts education. How can the interdisciplinary work of liberal studies, for example, bring harmony out of the dissonances of a curriculum, on the one hand, increasingly energized by the dynamic differences between races, classes, and genders, and a society, on the other, increasingly threatened by divisiveness, disengagement, and disenfranchisement? Can liberal studies help heal the wounds of our fractured national life? Or is the spirit of integration that has traditionally nourished myths of unity and consensus among interdisciplinary humanists more of a *problem* than a solution?

Benjamin DeMott (1990) accurately surveys such ethical ground. He questions our pressing need to bring alive the differences between us at a time when "our power to see others feelingly in their separateness and distinctness" is drained by a self-enclosure that grips moral life in America today. "There's too little realization," he complains, "that the first step

1

toward achieving the spirit of liberty is the development of a capacity to *believe* in difference and to register it, to imagine one's way deeply into the moment-to-moment feelings and attitudes of people placed differently from oneself" (13).

A report entitled "Democracy's Next Generation," issued by the non-partisan constitutional-liberties organization People for the American Way, concludes that among young Americans of all races between the ages of fifteen and twenty-four "self-interest often drowns out concern about our nation's progress toward full social equality. . . . Pulling back out of [an] economic fear" fueled by the media myth that living well is synonymous with material wealth, today's undergraduates, according to the report, "are remarkably pessimistic about our nation's future" (Kropp 1992, B3).

I detect a pessimism in some of my own students' moral discourses that stems, I believe, from increasing self-enclosure and, in particular, from the way that civic empathy and social idealism have lost their power to inspire the current generation's ethical commitments. In fact, many students today are frankly suspicious of idealism. Curiously, the word itself has undergone a shift in connotation and now means something slightly more akin to "fatalism" or "fantasy." The idealist is often viewed, then, as a sentimentalist or, worse, as a loser in a contemporary world where the future begins to look more like an inexorable grinding away of the present *into itself,* a world reawakened to an old nemesis of civic culture in America that the poet Langston Hughes decried as "the same old stupid plan / Of dog eat dog, of mighty crush the weak."

ETHICAL IDEALISM

I cannot draw this discussion into the labyrinth of idealism's many usages and meanings, since, as it has been said, the history of Western philosophy is largely a history of idealism, not to mention the parallel traditions that resonate powerfully in the philosophic and religious idealism of non-Western cultures, especially India and China. I am not as interested, however, in the philosophical character of idealism as much as with "ethical" or "social" idealism as it is most commonly understood in today's moral vernacular. According to this perspective, the notion of a society as a consortium of autonomous individuals is both absurd and destructive. Ethical idealism holds that persons are constituted by their networks of interaction with others, and an existence apart from those associations is, at best, a diminished existence. As such, there are ultimate, higher, suprapersonal "ideals" worth aspiring to—mutual welfare, for example, or social justice, or "enlightened" self-interest, or the empathic civility that is the ballast to jurist Learned Hand's spirit of liberty, "the spirit which seeks to understand the minds of other men and women without bias" (Hand 1952, 190).

Equally important, other-directed commitment, while serving the highest common good, is simultaneously the fulfillment of the individual. Ethical or social idealism, then, stakes the communitarian claim that individual moral freedom derives, not from psychological or natural necessity, not from filial or class arrangements, but from a covenant—whether secular or theistic—that binds the individual and the polity together into an ethical holism. In America that holism is a compact called "civil society," a compact that innervates our civic life and gives our national literature, no matter where we locate the canonical perimeters, its ethical urgency and its moral inspiration.

Ethical idealism is, if not the linchpin, at least a critical ingredient in the democratic humanism that makes civil society more than an entry in a dictionary of cultural literacy. It counts for something in the worlds of interpersonal relations, civic duty, work, and especially the vast terrain of self-reflection and self-purpose that all of us take a lifetime to survey. Reports like "Democracy's Next Generation" are particularly disheartening, then, in their implications that ethical idealism is such a low priority for young persons.

MORAL IMAGINATION AND THE SHAPE OF THE FUTURE

Few modern American plays better capture the essence of moral exuberance that galvanizes youthful idealism and idealistic action than Lorraine Hansberry's *A Raisin in the Sun*. Set against a backdrop of overt racism and pervasive housing discrimination during the 1950s, Hansberry's play manages both to recover and to sustain ethical idealism amid conditions that certainly warrant fatalistic surrender. And the play does so without sentimentality and in spite of the unresolved conflicts and uncertainties left over at the end, which remain Hansberry's legacy to the continuing struggle for racial justice and decency in America. It is a play about distress, futility, and tragedy, but also about hope and pride and what kind of conviction and commitment it takes to bring hope out of hopelessness, courage out of fear—in a word, idealism out of skepticism. Robert Coles (1986) describes the black family—the Youngers—and their ordeal in trying to move out of a segregated Chicago borough as a "continual tension between hope and despair in people who have had such a rough time and whose prospects are by no means cheerful" (60). Nowhere in the play is that tension more gripping than in the penultimate scene between Asagai and Beneatha Younger, a scene that Robert Nemiroff, who produced and adapted many of Hansberry's works, describes as capturing "the larger statement of the play—and the ongoing struggle it portends" (Hansberry 1987, x).

After Beneatha's brother, Walter Lee, squanders the portion of a life insurance claim set aside for Beneatha's medical education, she gives into despair, even cynicism, after watching her dream of becoming a doctor apparently go up in smoke. Beneatha had always pinned her personal aspirations along with her hopes for a more equable and compassionate society on the prospect of becoming a doctor, something that reflects Hansberry's belief that social idealism—the commitment to a better society—is intimately and inextricably tied to the problem of individual moral obligation: or, put differently, that social justice is the collective expression of an idealism held by and deeply felt among individuals. "I always thought," Beneatha says to Asagai, that being a doctor "was the one concrete thing in the world that a human being could do. Fix up the sick, you know—and make them whole again." Once the fragile

4

bond of commitment between an individual's aspirations and society's common welfare is broken, however, Beneatha quickly retrenches into cynicism.

I often detect this same cynicism coming from the struggling young voices in my own classrooms who feel so overwhelmed by the individual's powerlessness when faced with seemingly intractable social problems. Like my students, Beneatha wants to care. "I wanted to cure," she explains to Asagai. "It used to be so important to me. . . . I used to care. I mean about people and how their bodies hurt." When Asagai asks her to explain why she stopped caring, Beneatha comes to age, so to speak, morally. "Because [doctoring] doesn't seem deep enough, close enough to what ails mankind! It was a child's way of seeing things—or an idealist's."

It is at that point where the play pivots delicately on the moral fulcrum that Coles positions between hope and despair, or, in the social/ethical idiom of my own reading, between idealism and fatalism. Asagai, a patriot for an independent Africa, steps forward to defend hope and idealism. "Children," he reminds Beneatha, "see things very well sometimes—and idealists even better." Beneatha counters, bitterly cynical: "You with all your talk and dreams about [a free] Africa! You still think you can patch up the world. Cure the Great Sore of Colonialism—with the Penicillin of Independence—! . . . What about all the crooks and thieves and just plain idiots who will come into power and steal and plunder the same as before—only now they will be black . . .—WHAT ABOUT THEM?!"

Hansberry quickly synthesizes the moral dilemma into two very clear, precise geomoral images:

BENEATHA. . . Don't you see there isn't any real progress, Asagai, there is only one large circle that we march in, around and around, each of us with our own little picture in front of us—our own little mirage that we think is the future.

ASAGAI. . . It isn't a circle—it is simply a long line—as in geometry, you know, one that reaches into infinity. And because we cannot see the end—we also cannot see how it changes. And it is very odd but those who see the changes—who dream, who will not give up—are called idealists . . . and those who see only the circle—we call *them* the "realists."

These two contrasting images say it all. How one imagines the shape of the future—whether as another version of the present or as a limitless plain of possibilities for personal and societal change—determines moral action and ethical commitment. Hansberry makes her choice. Beneatha decides to become a doctor in Africa. The Younger family reaches down for the courage it takes to integrate a white neighborhood. Without getting into the important complexities and ambivalences of those decisions, we can say that they represent the courage and moral resourcefulness that were instrumental in and essential to the lasting successes of the following decade's civil rights struggles. Among liberals, for example, the Youngers' decision to move becomes the essence of what liberalism stood for during that time: namely, that the integration of American society was simultaneously the empowerment of black Americans and the salvation of white America. In his commentary on *A Raisin in the Sun,* Robert Nemiroff lifts the play to this higher level of sociomoral analysis.

> For at the deepest level it is not a specific situation but the human con-
> dition, human aspiration and human relationship—the persistence of
> dreams, of the bonds and conflicts between men and women, parents
> and children, old ways and new, and the endless struggle against human
> oppression, whatever the forms it may take, and for individual fulfill-
> ment, recognition, and liberation—that are at the heart of such plays. It
> is not surprising therefore that in each generation we recognize ourselves
> in them anew. (Hansberry, xvii–xviii)

GENERATIVITY

Erik Erikson's fascinating studies of Martin Luther (1962) and Mahatma Gandhi (1969) as young men reveal roughly the same dynamic pattern that emerges from Beneatha's search for self-fulfillment: idealism is a cru-cial component in a young person's necessary, natural, and humane conflict with the status quo. Not incidentally, the same is true for young women, as Carol Gilligan (1982), in spite of her differences with Erikson, shows in her work on moral development. As such, idealism is central to identity formation and indispensable to negotiating succeeding stages of the life cycle. Moral obligation—virtually synonymous, for Erikson, Gilligan, and Hansberry alike, with social idealism—is in fact the key to psychosocial maturity. Erikson (1968), for example, ranks obligation as the highest stage in the evolution of ethical life. What he terms "generativity"—"the concern for establishing and guiding the next generation"—is essential to the development of our inner resources, without which we risk losing our very "faith . . . and belief in the species." Moreover, "generativity," Erikson maintains, "is itself a driving force in human organization" (139). To be fully human, if I may simplify Erikson, is to be ethically concerned with and connected to the maintenance and betterment of the world.

Erikson's "generativity," then, is inseparable from an "idealism" that Asagai ascribes to "those [people] who dream, who will not give up" in their quests to make society a better place. And both are critical elements to identity formation—as Beneatha Younger discovers when she enthusiastically resolves to be "a doctor—in Africa!"—as well as to the development of moral literacy and civic empowerment.

Recalling the concerns expressed earlier by Benjamin DeMott and the People for the American Way over the social isolation and dystopian skepticism of young persons today, what is troubling is the apparent rupture between Erikson's "generativity" and much sense among today's undergraduates that commitment to a better society has anything at all to do with the work of self-discovery during a fertile period of identity formation coinciding with the college years. Skepticism over the possibilities for social progress betrays a surrender of students' allegiance to the next generation, a breach in what Erikson calls "the ethics of generative succession." It is almost as if they were snagged at that point in Beneatha's moral life when her identity as healer/doctor is suddenly aborted by Walter Lee's squandering the medical school tuition and she cynically mocks Asagai's idealistic pretensions—just at that point, in other words, when her personal aspirations and her societal commitments simultaneously unravel. Idealism and generative obligation, Erikson reminds us, are essential to such human dispositions as faith, purposefulness, fidelity, love, and care. Without them we stagnate; we are impoverished. Without them the future begins to look more like a circle, less like a long line of possibilities disappearing into infinity. Erikson gives us a choice in his dynamics of identity development between generativity or stagnation, between integrity or despair, between participation in the civic arena or retreat into a private sphere. But more important, as "criteria of vital individual strength," the altruistic drives, Erikson (1968) warns repeatedly in his psychohistorical studies, "also flow into the life of institutions. Without them, institutions wilt" (138).

Shut into the isolation of their skepticism and economic fear, today's students seem to be discounting hope for the continued vitality and viability of civil society in America along with the principles—the "ideals"—of tolerance, participation, and loyal dissent vital to the survival of its egalitarian institutions and central to traditions of liberal learning in its schools.

OUTSIDE THE MORAL ENCLOSURE

Robert Coles, one of Erik Erikson's most distinguished students, concurs with his former mentor that idealism is both psychologically empowering and socially useful. The kind of robust and inquiring idealism that Coles discovers in certain individuals reminds him how essential it is to be able to see beyond ourselves and to appreciate and value our stake in the dignity of others. The young secular idealists Coles writes about in his book *The Moral Life of Children* (1986) stand as stark—and, as such, perhaps unfair—contrasts to some of the more fatalistic skeptics among today's undergraduates. The social justice perspectives of Coles's civil rights volunteers and their moral discourses differ so much from today's students, in fact, that one is astonished at the values revolution that has occurred in the past two decades and a half. Coles notes, for example, that the degree of commitment among college-aged civil rights volunteers was so thoroughgoing and unrelenting that many faced crushing disillusionment when their high-minded efforts to completely wipe out racial prejudice among southern whites fell short.

That is nearly the opposite of the disillusionment many college students today fear: a disillusionment not of falling short of one's idealistic goals, but a disillusionment of getting entangled in the uncertain struggle for ideals in the first place—a disillusionment of outcome, in short, as opposed to a disillusionment of motive. Coles's example of a youthful idealism that risks disillusionment pinpoints the lasting moral content that self-enclosure robs today's students of:

> There is, at least in some of us, an intense idealism that doesn't yield its energy, late in life, to competing interests or obligations. Youthful idealism has become, for certain men and women, a much valued moral habit. Without it some middle-aged persons, even relatively old men or women, feel anxious or inadequate—or yes, even fearful. (198–199)

There are, to be sure, many student organizations today, and indeed many students, dedicated to the vitality of other-directed commitment that Coles found among civil rights volunteers during the early 1960s. Groups like Teach for America and Students for Appalachia come immediately to mind, in addition to hundreds of Service Learning Centers in colleges across the country that provide students with opportunities for meaningful and lasting public and community service. For the most part, however, the societal forces of opportunism and short-term gratification, along with the eclipse of idealism and what Christopher Lasch (1991) detects as "a particularly vicious kind of careerism" fostered by "society's icy indifference to everything that makes it possible for children to flourish and to grow up to be responsible adults" (33)—all of these force much different choices on most students today, choices, in the poet Philip Larkin's words, "to listen to money singing," choices that lead to the hideous spectacle of students attending baccalaureate exercises with For Sale signs hung around their necks and dollar bills glued to their mortarboards.

Students are not to blame for the crisis of self-enclosure. They are its victims. As David Purpel notes in an impassioned argument on *The Moral and Spiritual Crisis in Education* (1989), the "rigid and manic concerns with facilitating the individual pursuit of socioeconomic success" is a crisis endemic to educational institutions themselves and their "inability to make lasting and profound moral commitments that can energize and legitimize our [students'] day-to-day lives." The culture of mass education in America, he writes, "not only fail[s] to stem alienation" among students "but actually deepen[s] and widen[s] it" (56–57).

In our universities especially, professional humanities scholars for the most part have so completely abandoned public life in America that they no longer have a moral claim on solving its crises. Even our poets seem to have lost connection to a social world and the talent, as Edwin Muir (himself a "public poet") said, "to turn outward." "That we have no poets," writes Wendell Berry (1983), "who are . . . public persons suggests even more forcibly the weakness of our poetry. . . . In his protest, the contemporary poet is speaking publicly, but not as a spokesman; he is only one outraged citizen speaking *at* other citizens who do not know him, whom he does not know, and with whom he does not sympathize" (20). Increasingly, we have to turn elsewhere—to Latin America, Central Europe, China—for a national literature, as the Russian poet Yevgeny Yevtushenko puts it, where "poetry and literature nurture idealism."

We are in crisis. Vartan Gregorian (1989), in his inaugural address as president of Brown University, appealed to both students and faculty to break out of what he called "the pygmy world of private piety" where we have all become "social, political, and moral isolationists."

> We have no choice but to end the imprisonment of the self and concern ourselves with those outside our moral enclosure. We need a moral center, not a moral enclosure. We need to be capable of moral outrage and sensitive to the pain and sorrow of our fellow man and woman. It is important not only to be able to engage in new ideas, but also be willing to make public declarations of one's convictions and commitments and then translate them into actions and deeds. (34)

10

INTRAGENERATIONAL CONFLICT

The difficulty we have in translating Gregorian's commitments into meaningful social action brings us back to the basic issue of moral literacy and the ambivalences we face over moral terms such as *idealism*. Certainly, intergenerational conflicts contribute no little to that confusion, especially as the fault lines of a new generation gap are pried open by growing antiboomer animosity among so-called Generation Xers (Howe and Straus 1992). Young persons today are turned off by calls, like Gregorian's, to breach the moral enclosure of contemporary life because previous generations failed to make much of the "ethics of generative succession." We should not gloss over such intergenerational dimensions of our values crisis. But neither should we minimize the *intragenerational* divisions that complicate our students' dilemmas of commitment, conflicts that make it no easier for them to decide whether to retreat into "private piety" or risk the tenuous rewards of life and work outside Gregorian's "moral enclosure."

That intragenerational conflict was particularly well illustrated on a segment of the *MacNeil/Lehrer News Hour*, one in a series of programs ("Evaluating the 80's") that aired in December 1989 and offered reflections on the past decade and commentaries on prospects for the 1990s. This particular broadcast (December 26, 1989) brought together five college students from across the country for a fascinating exchange of views "on what," as Jim Lehrer proposed in his introduction, "this last decade has wrought." After the dialogue turned to the uncomfortable issue of the current college generation's self-absorption, Laurie Broquet, a student at Oakland Community College in Michigan, argued with the position taken by another panelist that today's college students, as he put it, have "to be out for themselves more" because society has become so competitive. Ms. Broquet disagreed. "I think college students have a large role and a big responsibility to go back into their communities," she countered, and "stress the importance of education, the importance of understanding your country, about your history, about the future, about technology, about computers, which is our future, the goals of our country and the world." Her comments elicited the following exchange where "idealism," as a moral term, takes on familiar dichotomous connotations.

MR. BAUMGARTNER: That's incredibly idealistic for her to think you have that much time to do that. A lot of us have to work our way through school and to say we have time just to go out and teach people values at the drop of a hat is just incredibly idealistic I think.

Ms. KOCH: I think it may be idealistic, but if we, who are the leaders of the world in the next generation can't be idealistic, I don't know who can be. I mean, we need to take our values and our standards and we need to be idealistic with them and to try and teach others the importance of public service, the importance of getting a good education, of not doing drugs, and also I'm bringing a larger world view to it, but also the importance of democracy and pluralism as we're seeing going on in the rest of the world. I think we need to be idealistic. I think it's important.

It would be wonderful to stop the tape at that point and start digging into the roots of Mr. Baumgartner's and Ms. Koch's moral vocabularies and question them about their use of idealism and get right to the connotations informing their disagreement. I think we would uncover a collision of meanings that reveal a fundamental moral conflict between virtue and expediency. Obviously, these two panelists pitch completely different topspins on their moral diction. Mr. Baumgartner uses "idealistic" in a mildly pejorative way to criticize Ms. Broquet's position. He is taking a page from a moral lexicon where idealism fades into skepticism. For Mr. Baumgartner idealism interferes with competition. The idealist, in other words, runs the risk of ending up on the short end of the stick in the race to get ahead. Ms. Koch is familiar with that connotation. But she quickly subordinates it to a consensual understanding that, as Erikson and Coles remind us, views idealism from a different moral vantage point as *principled action in the world*. She uses idealism in its generative sense as duty, responsibility, obligation, virtue. Her understanding carries the ethical burden of those qualities Erikson identifies as generativity and integrity. And her retort to Mr. Baumgartner underscores a quiet intragenerational conflict over the consequences, I suspect, of his use of idealism that evokes Erikson's alternatives: namely, stagnation and despair.

At the very least, the exchange between these two panelists illustrates a fundamental moral ambivalence students face today: an idealism, like Ms. Koch's, that empowers moral choice—that animates, as John Dewey (1939) remarked, the very breath of life—struggles to reconcile an idealism, like Mr. Baumgartner's, completely isolated from praxis.

MORAL ECOLOGY AND THE AMERICAN DREAM

How to restore Ms. Koch's brand of social idealism as a moral habit is the single most critical challenge facing interdisciplinary teaching humanists today. Without a real capacity among students to *believe* in difference, a multicultural curriculum may not be much improvement over the universally discredited Anglocentric course of study. No matter how daunting or frustrating the challenge to inspire generative concern in students without caving into moralism might be, we don't have the liberty to defer the job. John Dewey, whose pragmatist social psychology established the benchmark for moral education and civic literacy in modern America, reminds us in the durable *Democracy and Education* (1939) that "interest in community welfare, an interest that is intellectual and practical, as well as emotional—an interest, that is to say, in perceiving whatever makes for social order and progress, and in carrying these principles into execution—is the moral habit to which all the special school habits must be related if they are to be animated by the breath of life" (627). That is exactly what Vartan Gregorian had in mind when he challenged Brown University undergraduates to temper their privileged destinies with Tocqueville's "enlightened self-interest": "It is incumbent upon us as moral and spiritual beings," Gregorian exhorted, "to distinguish between integrity and compromise, justice and injustice, personal gain and public interest, means and ends, good and evil" (35).

Today, more than ever before, we need a perceptive, critical, concerned, and questioning citizenry capable of making such distinctions, particularly among those young persons currently negotiating the crucial, and never before so rocky, transition into adulthood. In a world of rapidly changing interglobal politics where fledgling democracies teeter delicately between civic empowerment and civil disorder, it may be fatal for American students to view the "real world" as static, monolithic, and unchangeable. John le Carré, an astute novelist with a wonderful eye for interglobal complexity, assesses the nature of the *real* "real world" we face today in a *New York Times* op-ed piece (1989). He writes that we are on the verge of "a unique moment in history—perhaps no longer than the blink of a star—when to be a realist it is necessary also to be an idealist, when the improbable is happening every day and the impossible every week, and where imagination and creativity, unleashed in time, may yet sweep us above the slough of hopelessness we have been condemned to too long" (A35).

Some have said that in an age of consumption the role of concerned citizen has long since given way to that of the savvy consumer, maybe in the same way that, for so many students, the idealist has surrendered to the skeptic. If so, nothing less than a revolutionary way of thinking about and relating to the world may be necessary in a civic pedagogy particularly well suited to interdisciplinary methodologies that have always been drawn to borders, margins, frontiers, and unexplored territories. The authors of *Habits of the Heart* refer to one such mode of interdisciplinary inquiry and thinking as "moral ecology." "Human beings and their societies," the authors write, "are deeply interrelated, and the actions we take have enormous ramifications for the lives of others" (Bellah et al. 1985, 284). Moral ecology recognizes that interrelatedness. Thus, our moral vocabulary needs to regain its linguistic bearings as a language of otherness and interrelatedness. Moral terms such as idealism and aspiration and freedom and the pursuit of happiness must resonate into a world of principled action and not become suffocated by skepticism among isolated selves cut off from the subtle and myriad ties that bind people together whether we choose to recognize them or not.

Even so, the stubborn and persistent myth of the American Dream continues springing back to life and dampening social awareness with self-serving visions of the material good life that impact civic literacy and civic responsibility, as evidenced by the fact that more people voted in the recent Elvis postage stamp plebiscite than in some municipal elections and more homes were tuned to a rerun of *Roseanne* than the combined audience for

14

all three commercial networks' coverage of a political party convention last June. Robert Bellah and coauthors (1985) succinctly circumscribe the myth as follows:

> The American dream is often a very private dream of being the star, the uniquely successful and admirable one, the one who stands out from the crowd of ordinary folk who don't know how. And since we have believed in that dream for a long time and worked very hard to make it come true, it is hard for us to give it up, even though it contradicts another dream that we have—that of living in a society that would really be worth living in. (285)

TIES THAT BIND

The resilience of that socially corrosive myth is astonishing. We persist using a moral ecology tuned to acquisition, consumption, and material prosperity even as our natural ecology is irreparably damaged by the mass production of disposable junk and our social ecology is scarred by homelessness, illiteracy, malnutrition, unemployment, and underemployment in an increasingly degrading service economy. There are those who would have our morality and moral language follow the mysterious trajectory of a self-regulating market, and our moral imaginations spring to life out of the arid sands of skepticism. There are others who remind us, either explicitly or implicitly, that the market and its empowering myth of the American Dream is a wonderful servant but a disastrous master—others who, like Ms. Koch, "need to be idealistic," who "think it's important."

REFERENCES

Bellah, Robert, Richard Madsen, William Sullivan, Ann Swindler, and Steven Tipton. 1985. *Habits of the Heart: Individualism and Commitment in American Life.* Berkeley: University of California Press.

Berry, Wendell. 1983. *Standing By Words.* San Francisco: North Point.

Botstein, Leon. 1990. "Damaged Literacy: Illiteracies and American Democracy." *Daedalus* 119.2: 55–84.

Coles, Robert. 1986. *The Moral Life of Children.* Boston: Houghton.

DeMott, Benjamin. 1990. *The Imperial Middle: Why Americans Can't Think Straight About Class.* New York: Morrow.

Dewey, John. 1939. *Intelligence in the Modern World: John Dewey's Philosophy.* Ed. Joseph Ratner. New York: Modern Library.

Erikson, Erik. 1962. *Young Man Luther.* New York: Norton.

———. 1968. *Identity: Youth and Crisis.* New York: Norton.

———. 1969. *Gandhi's Truth.* New York: Norton.

Gilligan, Carol. 1982. *In a Different Voice: Psychological Theory and Women's Development.* Cambridge: Harvard University Press.

Gregorian, Vartan. 1989. "Three Challenges for Higher Education." *Brown University Alumni Magazine*, May: 31–35.

Hand, Learned. 1952. *The Spirit of Liberty.* Ed. Irving Dilliard. New York: Alfred Knoph.

Hansberry, Lorraine. 1987. *A Raisin in the Sun.* New York: Signet.

Howe, N., and W. Straus. 1992. "The New Generation Gap." *Atlantic Monthly*, December.

Kropp, Arthur J. 1992. "Colleges Must Find Ways to Eradicate Racial Divisions." *Chronicle of Higher Education*, April 22: B3–B4.

Lasch, Christopher. 1991. *The True and Only Heaven: Progress and Its Critics.* New York: Norton.

le Carré, John. 1989. "Why I Came in From the Cold." *New York Times*, September 29: A35.

Purpel, David. 1989. *The Moral and Spiritual Crisis in Education: A Curriculum of Justice and Compassion in Education.* Granby, MA: Bergin.

MORAL LITERACY (1994)

ONE OF MY PRINCIPAL CONCERNS AS A WRITING TEACHER IS MY STU-
dents' moral literacy and, in particular, the critical nexus formed in the
writing classroom by language, moral sensibility, cultural values, identity
development, and ethical behavior. I am well aware of how slippery and
risky the term "moral literacy" can be. I do not mean necessarily to imply
an individual's talent or acumen for judging right from wrong merged with
the language arts. Nor would I endorse William Kilpatrick's problematic
flip side of the term used in his recent study of the public school's "moral
weightlessness," subtitled *Moral Illiteracy and the Case for Character Education* (1992). Moral literacy encompasses, instead, the discourse imagery
we use to articulate aspiration, commitment, and identity—in Lionel Trilling's (1979) phrase, our "images of personal being"—as we search for inner
meaning and truth within the context of interpersonal commitments and
wider obligations to society. Intrinsic to higher learning, "moral literacy," as
Alexis de Tocqueville (1945) understood, means that an "instruction which
enlightens the understanding is not [to be] separated from [a] moral education which amends the heart" (190). I concur, then, with William Damon's
(1990) assessment of "moral literacy" as "the best route to, and the finest
social purpose for, the higher forms of literacy" (51). As the historian of
rhetoric James Berlin (1984) has said, "When we teach students to write

we are teaching more than an instrumental skill. We are teaching a mode of conduct, a way of responding to experience" (86) that "causes reverberations in all features of a student's private and social behavior" (92).

During a recent class session, my students and I got into an argument over "idealism" that illustrates how frustrating and slippery the concept of moral literacy can be. My students and I were discussing the Declaration of Independence and Langston Hughes's poem "Let America Be America Again." In that poem Hughes presents starkly contrasting ethical perspectives on the Declaration's "pursuit of happiness" blocked in against a history of racial discrimination: the rugged individualist credo, as Hughes puts it, "of dog eat dog, of mighty crush the weak" versus the egalitarian vision contained in Thomas Jefferson's democratic humanism. I had asked my students to consider Jefferson's civic republican principles—liberty, social justice, collective self-determination, and so on—and the virtues accompanying them (e.g., toleration, respect for differences, selflessness) in light of Hughes's sobering reassessment of such principles and virtues from an African American perspective just at the dawning of the civil rights movement. My point was to discuss openly these conflicting visions of national purpose, then seek to reconcile the collision of images in the poem, hopefully along with the ethical freight carried by those images. How we resolve the poem's central moral dilemma—privilege and power versus egalitarianism in a democracy—tells us, I believed (and still do), something about our own moral lives and how we handle the problem of obligation—the linchpin of moral life—and what moral vocabulary best informs those solutions.

In spite of such lofty aims (or, upon further reflection, maybe *because* of them), it was one of those sessions when you work a class into a knot of disagreements and finally cross a threshold where no one really listens anymore. No reconciliations. No resolutions. My well-worn concept of idealism, in effect, boomeranged on me, along with the pedagogical gambit I had yoked it to. It occurred to me only after class ended that the reason the session fizzled was that my students and I had entirely different connotations for the word. I had tripped unknowingly over what William Damon (1990) describes as a discontinuity of generational commitments, a classic values mismatch, according to Damon, between the moral literacies of generations. Frankly, I had expected students to solve a moral problem as I would and, along with Hughes, condemn "the same old stupid plan / Of dog eat dog, of mighty crush the weak" in favor of Hughes's geomoral imagery of America as a "great strong land of love / Where never kings connive nor tyrants scheme / That any man be crushed by one above." But students were more fatalistically inclined. They did not share Hughes' optimism over idealism as socially transformative, nor did they as strongly oppose biological, filial, and economic determinism as disvalues. Commitment to a better society may still carry some vestigial freight in the civic rituals of American public life, as illustrated most recently by Senator Bill Bradley's dramatic evocation of "Let America Be America Again" in a keynote speech before the Democratic National Convention (July 14, 1992). But if my students' pessimism over the possibilities for social change is any indication, social idealism, it would seem, lands with a thud in private life.

Simply put, to me Langston Hughes's poem is about a social idealism that innervates civic commitment. To my students, the poem is about power, about what they have come to accept uncritically as "the real world" and its trenchant determinism. I detect in my students' response to the poem the same evolution in both ethical perspective and moral diction that Leon Botstein claims is inevitable as linguistic change accompanies a change in collective moral thinking. He uses the example of how the word "hope" has evolved in common usage from a predicate—as in "I hope America can be a 'land where every[one] is free'"—to an adverb—as in "Hopefully, America can be a 'land where every[one] is free.'" The predicate construction, Botstein writes, "carries with it the assumption of personal responsibility to act on hope and express the potential of utility in hoping, speaking, and acting." The newer adverbial form, in contrast, "signals the idea that what happens is the result of neither one's beliefs nor one's actions, that one is powerless and subject to amorphous circumstances and impersonal forces apart from one's existence. The current use of hopefully reduces hope to a mere feeling," Botstein continues, "an emotion, a sentiment which is at once vague and inarticulate. Therefore one is impotent to realize in the present and future any aspiration implied by hope." My students' point of view on Hughes's poem and the connotations that inform their usage of "idealism" seem to have followed a not dissimilar pattern: a distancing, that is to say, from personal responsibility in the face of social injustice, which leaves most students reading Hughes's agitation as resentment, rage, and frustration. William Damon (1990) understands that pattern of change as a discontinuity of generational moral literacies. And Leon Botstein (1990) judges the change as both a linguistic impoverishment and a moral loss. "In the shift," Botstein concludes, "one can perceive a weakening of faith in personal efficacy, a pessimism and an exhaustion—a sense of the superfluity of individual belief and influence" (1990, 80–81).

Classic research in the fields of rhetoric and composition theory holds that language proficiency, critical thinking skills, and moral reasoning develop symbiotically. Increased linguistic dexterity and virtuosity have long been understood to be closely associated not only with cognitive development but with refinements in the entire conceptual triad of moral development as well: namely, moral judgment, moral behavior, and moral emotion. A new generation of literacy experts and a new wave of culture critics, however, reject the term "moral literacy" out of hand. Their quarrel with a concept that yokes together language acquisition, language competency, and moral development follows two basic lines of dissent concerning, first, how we understand literacy and what it means to be a literate person, and second, the definitions, political contexts, ideological ramifications, and precise connotative topspin one puts on the word "morality" as such.

LITERACY AND INDOCTRINATION

Among contemporary literacy theorists, the most potent criticism comes from those who adopt what Brian Street has called an "ideological model" of literacy, a group whose position is best stated by Street himself in *Literacy in Theory and Practice*, a landmark study first published in 1984. This model views literacy as a dynamic social process. "It assumes," according to Street, "that the meaning of literacy depends upon the social institutions in which it is embedded." Moreover, literacy is highly charged with political and ideological significance. Literacy cannot be understood as separate from those contextual significances and treated, as Street says, "as though it were an 'autonomous' thing" (8). According to the ideological model, then, the danger is that moral literacy, both practically and conceptually, must be acknowledged as an instrument of social control that imposes upon students prevailing sociomoral categories and political conditions. In doing so, it inevitably co-opts the autonomous integrity of moral language in a cultural-linguistic tradition that stresses freedom of speech as a weapon of critical dissent. Such a position is compatible with Damon, Botstein, and other linguistic contextualists' sensitivity to literacy's strong social bearings, but clearly inconsistent with what they understand to be the consequences of what it means—and what it feels like—to be a literate person. Instead of an instrument of control that raises the troubling specter of social manipulation, moral literacy can be viewed as a pathway to responsible ethical commitment that liberates students for rewarding and meaningful practices of personal commitment and social obligation—practices that can effectively counter ideological and political hegemonies as much as copy or be duped by them.

I am marginally sympathetic to the ideological model because, for the most part, its theoretical alternative is considerably more disingenuous in its claims for objectivity and ideological neutrality. What Street labels the "autonomous model" differs little from Myron Tuman's definition of an "unproblematic model" (1987, 9–11) of literacy that stresses only the practical concerns of language development—such as the measurable proficiency of a student's coding skills—and the autonomous and parallel, but independent, developmental relationship between literacy and socialization. The autonomous or unproblematic model, usually associated with the work of social anthropologist Jack Goody (1977), rests on the assumption that literacy, as Brian Street explains, "is a neutral technology that can be detached from specific social contents" (1): literacy, in short, is a value-free "technology of the intellect" and "unproblematic" with respect to its vulnerability to ideological manipulation or coercion. The autonomous model sees literacy as only remotely connected to social processes and more closely associated with cognitive refinements like objectivity, abstraction, speculation, logic, cost-benefit analysis, and the ability to connect hypotheses, all common to what Goody and others have referred to as the more advanced "alphabetic cultures." Advocates of the autonomous model tend to discount as "problematic" the development of higher order discourse skills in social contexts along with the relationship between language, self-image, and moral agency.

Street's and Tuman's critique of the autonomous model is credible. The autonomous model is not, in effect, either autonomous or entirely "value-free." Any attempt to dissociate language use and mental skills from cultural conventions and social processes is disingenuous and highly "problematic" because it is itself ideological and laden with values.

For example, the current agitation in the United States for basic literacy programs, spurred by plummeting test scores, reveals a functional literacy paradigm freighted with orientations to thought processes and cognitive skills that suit and serve a particular model of achievement, bureaucratic procedure, technical acumen, and style that cannot be passed off as value-free. Those who favor the autonomous model, Street contends, are not appealing to objectivity and values neutrality. They are "privileging" an ideological and institutional bias toward objectivity and value-free neutrality. The autonomous model's claims for literacy are themselves, in a word, ideological claims. "They are part of an armoury of concepts, conventions, and practices," Street writes, "that give meaning to and protect the writers' own social formation and specifically their own place within it. What [its advocates] are privileging and providing ideological support for is, in fact, their own academic establishment, their own work practice within it, their own values and rules" (38).

LITERACY AND LIBERATION

Where I part company with hard-line advocates of the ideological model is over their inflexible postulate that all practices of reading, writing, and critical discourse learning are taught to reinforce social and class stratification. Given the political/social/cultural matrix of literacy development, must it necessarily follow, as hard-liners maintain, that language acquisition and instruction are always and everywhere repressive? I simply don't believe, as Street contends, that literacy programs are "restrictive and hegemonic, and concerned with instilling discipline and exercising social control" (18), even though I have no problem with the notion that literacy is a practice embedded in society and culture, and I realize that literacy campaigns have been, and are, used as propaganda tools. To view literacy, however, as culturally specific and simultaneously oppressive strikes me as hardheaded, claustrophobic in its reductionism, or, frankly, paranoid. To presuppose that all literacy practices are inherently repressive because they seek to colonize a certain ideological version of the status quo tends to entirely exclude the possibility that language can carry a culture's impress in ways that empower and liberate persons rather than oppress or subjugate them. Language is capable of embracing the most important dimensions of our moral situations as individuals and, in this way, may guide us to react to our social conditions with empathy and critical insight instead of a cynicism and distrust that strike me as inevitable by-products of the strict social constructionist view of moral literacy.

MORALITY OR MORALISM?

One reason why critics find the marriage of morality and literacy repugnant or risky is, I believe, partly definitional. How one defines "morality" seems far more contentious than disagreements that may arise over what one means by a literate person and the process used to achieve literacy. This is especially true during the current climate of prevailing poststructural thought when the word "morality" itself provokes such a prickly response among the critical intelligentsia. In *Literacy and the Survival of Humanism* (1983), for example, Richard Lanham makes a formidable argument in favor of completely dissociating moral reasoning from language and literacy pedagogy. "Perhaps people will always talk about language in moral terms," Lanham concedes, "since it is so much more enjoyable that way, but we ought not to elaborate this practice," he warns, "into a pedagogy" (105). His concerns are essentially twofold. The moral context, first, over-simplifies human motives, Lanham believes, by wrenching persons "out of the complex setting which makes . . . behavior intelligible" (82). A "more intelligible context," according to Lanham, is the sociobiological quarter where such things as behavior, learning, and communication are played out in their full range of complexities. "You have to take the discussion [of rhetoric and literacy] out of its moralizing context and put it in a behavioral one" (59). In short, the moral context, Lanham believes, is too constricting and unsophisticated, too narrowly circumscribed. The complexities of rhetoric and literacy require, instead, a tripartite theory of human motivation spanning "play, game, and purpose" instead of the one-dimensional field of moral value alone. Second, Lanham brings a characteristic post-modern skepticism to the presumed authoritarianism and absolutism that, for some, moral agency implies. "No point," he asserts simply, ought to be "morally superior" (63) to another. For someone like Lanham—who has directed a highly regarded college-level writing program—it hardly follows, however, that no literacy pedagogy (no matter whether it stresses function, ideology, socialization, or developmental and behavioral processes) ought to be thought of as qualitatively superior to another. It is one thing to chide the moral dimension in theoretical ruminations over rhetoric and sociobiology, quite another to impose widely accepted, and quite acceptable, standards of achievement on student writing practices. An obvious parallel suggests a similar confusion among those professors today who loudly decry the oppressive practices of a traditional curriculum while happily lecturing students and grading their performances in the classroom.

Lanham's dismissal of morality from discussions of human motive follows from his apparent endorsement, one suspects, of what Alasdair MacIntyre calls "emotivism." MacIntyre defines emotivism as a doctrine in which all evaluative and normative judgments are nothing but assertions of personal preference, attitude, or feeling. "If and insofar as emotivism is true," MacIntyre says, "moral language is seriously misleading and, if and insofar as emotivism is justifiably believed, presumably the use of traditional and inherited moral language ought to be abandoned" (1984, 20). Doubtless Lanham is a believer. After all, the moral perspective, he writes, "plunks . . . [human behavior] in a context of plain [moral] purpose where it seems quite mad" (81). Even worse, the moral perspective brought to bear on literacy practices threatens, Lanham fears, to degenerate writing instruction into "a vehemence of religious disputation." For those arbiters of language who "construe their tasks in moral terms," Lanham suggests, "the only question to be asked of language use is 'Right or Wrong.' This moral premise distorts every question asked in its name" (91).

Lanham, it seems to me, is talking more about antipathy to "dogmatism" than he is about "morality." If I could substitute the word "moral" with the more accurate term "axiomatic" in all the passages quoted above, I'd be in complete agreement with him. But for the time being, let's grant Lanham his point: morality oversimplifies the complexities of human motive and purpose. Moreover, the moral perspective in discussions about literacy threatens to violate the emotivist credo that no point ought to be morally superior to another because all normative judgments are based on feelings and preferences anyway, not on first principles, ultimate concerns, or inalienable truths.

That latter point recalls Brian Street and the trepidations of those who advocate the ideological model of literacy. Like Lanham, when Street uses "morality" he does so to describe prescriptive behaviors and coercive practices. "The moral, socializing function of literacy teaching," then, becomes indistinguishable from "a narrowing [learning] experience aimed at inculcating the moral norms and disciplines of the ruling class" (1984, 108–109). For Street and Lanham, such phrases as "political coercion," "social control," "indoctrination," and "ideological hegemony" are perfectly interchangeable with "moral bases of behavior," "moral codes," and "moral principles."

My question: shouldn't *moral literacy* be subject to a relaxing of the same totalizing claims that Wayne Booth (1988) appeals to in his call for the rejuvenation of ethical criticism in English studies? "If ethical criticism of narrative," Booth writes, "is once again to find a place for itself, it must avoid the loaded labels and crude slogans that critics preoccupied with moral effects have too often employed" (7).

MORAL VISION

In his extraordinary book *The Moral Life of Children* (1986), Robert Coles tells a story about a remarkable Brazilian boy, a story that might survey more neatly morality's definitional boundaries and help resolve the territorial dispute between Lanham, Street, MacIntyre, and Booth over the consequences of moral terminology. Coles spent several days interviewing and tagging along with Eduardo, a destitute ten-year-old who lives in a squalid, ramshackle ghetto cobbled together along a steep foothill overlooking Rio de Janeiro and the bustling pavements of the Copacabana where Eduardo hustles a living. The boy comes to embody for Coles one of the great puzzles of moral character, the same puzzle George Orwell encountered when he struggled to explain the dignity, the humility, the ability to bear such awful burdens among English miners he visited in the 1930s and wrote about in *The Road to Wigan Pier*, the same puzzle that snagged James Agee when he lived among southern sharecroppers, a moral puzzle that combusted into the tortured poetry of *Let Us Now Praise Famous Men*. The gentle, unassuming boy forces the American psychiatrist to question the "origins of moral character," "the reasons why people end up as they do." How does one explain, for example, Eduardo's extraordinary sensitivity to others? What accounts for his "subtle intelligence," Coles wonders, his "compassionate regard for others, even those who are rich and powerful and seemingly insensitive to his own kind" (103), indeed those who have elbowed Eduardo and thousands of benighted Brazilians beyond the very margins of human indecency to a favela within eyeshot of the luxury hotels and string bikini boutiques along the beaches at Ipanema?

> Eduardo is among Brazil's poor, yet he has not lost what I suppose can be called moral pride, a kind of self-respect that even a ten-year-old scurrying across the hot pavements of the Copacabana can manage to possess. But whence comes such a quality? Why is it absent in others? . . . Why is it that some people who bear awful pain turn out to be so very nice whereas others turn out not so nice at all, or worse? (105–106)

Such questions ignite page after page of intense searching as Coles enters Eduardo's moral life and explores his "moral assumptions and purposes—what he believes to be 'right,' and what he believes to be terribly 'wrong,' and how he came to have and to hold dear those distinctions" (103). But the closer Coles gets to the magnetic poles of the boy's moral compass and the source of Eduardo's prescriptions for moral behavior and his moral attitude, the more the entire conceptual framework of morality as a proscriptive agency becomes insubstantial and ambiguous. The puzzle of Eduardo's morality, in other words, derives, Coles realizes, from a clinician's perspective that confines morality to an evaluative faculty, as opposed to a documentarian's vantage point that otherwise frees Coles to participate fully, and feelingly, in the boy's moral life. In a sense, then, Eduardo teaches Coles very little about the origins of moral character and much more about empathy, the proper questions for human morality as such, and especially the need to eschew rigid formulas when assessing moral actions and, in particular, to check the impulse to reduce morality to the simple business of discriminating between right and wrong. Coles discovers the richness and complexity of Eduardo's moral life not in the moral decisions that Eduardo makes but rather in his courage and his conviction, his way of seeing himself in relation to a personal world of deprivation and endless hustle and a social world of gruesome economic realities and cruel economic ironies, and, especially, in the language that permits Eduardo, as Coles says, to be "reflective about his family, himself, and, not the least, his future" (102).

> Will any summary of this boy's "mental status" bring us closer to understanding what in his decade of life on this planet has made him what he is? . . . The boy's "qualities" have been secured in the face of the awful wretchedness of a family's continuing ordeals. . . . All he can do, then, is persist, hope, try all the angles a mind will let him try. But those angles are shaped by another angle—one of vision: the possibilities and restrictions, both, which a particular moral sensibility evokes in time. (111–112)

Coles's experience with Eduardo reminds us that morality has more to do with aspiration, hope, "vision," and a person's ability, or indeed refusal, to transcend the exigencies of social station and existential circumstance than it does with rules that sanction or prescribe certain behaviors and taboos that prohibit others, those "platitudes" and "premises" that Richard Lanham dismisses because they "distort every question asked in [their] name" and those coercive principles that Brian Street cautions against as instruments of social control. When using the word morality, then, we need to think about those enabling principles that reveal to persons ontological possibilities, not behavioral constraints, and help them distinguish between the meaningful and the meaningless, the purposeful and the purposeless, the worthwhile and the worthless. As we construct meaningful moral distinctions as templates of moral behavior, we need not condemn the worthless, the meaningless, the purposeless, and so on, as either immoral, wrong, or taboo, as hard-line moralists might claim. Instead, morality, as I understand it, provides us with meaningful resources to carry ourselves into the worlds of learning, work, and love with ideals we can act on and make real, with ways to define our relationship to the world, to act and interact in that world, and to shape our destinies, aspirations, hopes, purposes, callings, and commitments. Robert Coles uses morality in this sense when he writes warmly, but not cloyingly, of the tragedies of children like Eduardo and their "bold moral confrontations" with social forces grounded in power, rapacity, selfishness, and greed. For these children, "moral purpose . . . become[s] a stoic's resigned acceptance of the tragic possibilities both life and death offer us. . . . [T]hese children live near or precisely on the edge. Having shunned (in fear, in disgust, in anxiety) the depraved life of which they see plenty, they seem to take the other way as an existential alternative, a moral inheritance" (133–134).

MORALITY AND IDENTITY

A final look at Lawrence Kohlberg's schema for understanding moral orientations will further fine-tune definitional boundaries. Kohlberg's summary of primary interpretive categories typically used in moral philosophy establishes more precisely what Coles means by morality and how that meaning might differ in critical perspective from Brian Street and Richard Lanham.

Kohlberg (1976), a major figure in the psychology of moral development, describes four basic orientations toward understanding moral behavior. The "normative order" considers human morality a response to prescribed rules, an orientation toward roles inscribed in the social order. In the "normative order," moral behavior is less reactive and more reflexive; it is understood as a decision-making process in which "right action" conforms to socially prescribed standards external to the self. The second category concerns what Kohlberg labels the "utility consequences" of moral action; morality is oriented to the "good and bad welfare consequences" that obtain from a given decision and its impact on others or on the self. In this case, moral decision-making is more reactive, less reflexive. Concepts of "justice and fairness" key the third category into interpersonal contracts where moral actions are governed by exchange or cost-benefit relations such as equality, reciprocity, or duty. In Kohlberg's third category, moral behavior is understood more in terms of responsibilities negotiated prior to moral action, and not as a reaction or reflex to cues or consequences that might follow.

Kohlberg bases the final category on the way that moral agency helps shape identity in response to a self-image internalized in what he calls an "ideal-self." Kohlberg describes this last mode as "an orientation to an image of [the] actor as a *good self,* or as someone with a conscience, and to his motives or virtue (relatively independent of approval consequences from others)" (40). As an orientation to an "ideal-self," morality can now be understood less in behavioral terms and more in ontological terms and especially in aesthetic terms insofar as moral discourse becomes the primary narrative of the "ideal-self." In addition to its ontological and aesthetic functions, morality in Kohlberg's fourth orientation carries a teleological component. That is to say, not only do moral decisions dispose us toward practices that fulfill identity in response to an "ideal-self," but also, as Alasdair MacIntyre puts it, morality "sustain[s] us in the relevant kind of quest for the good, by enabling us to overcome the harms, dangers, temptations and distractions which we encounter, and which will furnish us with increasing self-knowledge and increasing knowledge of the good" (219). This final category is more consistent with classical concepts of morality, as noted by both Kohlberg and MacIntyre, and less compatible with legalistic, utilitarian, or political connotations carried by the first three classifications. Tracing its roots, for example, to Greek and Latin etymological antecedents, MacIntyre reports that morality "means 'pertaining to character,' where a [person]'s character is nothing other than . . . set dispositions to behave systematically in one way rather than another, to lead one particular kind of life" (38).

When I speak of "moral literacy," then, I am defining morality within the framework of Kohlberg's fourth category. Unlike Lanham and Street, who are clearly more concerned with the "normative order" and the "utility consequences" of morality, I understand morality as a complex interaction between processes of identity formation, the development of social conscience, and the practice of actions that dispose individuals toward "virtue" in the classic sense—to "knowledge," that is to say, of "the good." I am particularly concerned with aesthetic ramifications where moral language reveals much about the "ideal-self" and how it interprets and articulates ethical practices and actions in narrative form as expectations, aspirations, attitudes, and beliefs. I do not bring to morality the trepidations that Richard Lanham and Brian Street have over morality's utility consequences, nor do I completely share their understandable fear that morality might impose rigorous standards of justice and fairness based on a collective will to power, rather than on individuals' empathy or the complex relations of equality and reciprocity that mediate interpersonal relations and compel social commitments. I am less concerned, then, with *prescriptive morality* in either Street's strict political or ideological sense (in which morality is an instrument for social control) or Lanham's canonical sense (in which morality is best understood as "moralism"). I am less concerned with laws, rules, and taboos, and more interested in narratives, images, metaphors of conviction and commitment; less with authority, punishment, coercion, and restriction, more with affection, empathy, civility, trust, justice, and possibility; less with property rights and ideological territoriality than with human values that sometimes cannot be completely understood in the contractual terms of cost-benefit analyses and power exchanges.

I am concerned, in short, with the aesthetic character of human morality and, in turn, with the character of a moral discourse that struggles— sometimes pathetically, sometimes beautifully, rarely with complete facility or perfection—to articulate Kohlberg's "ideal-self." Louis Raths, a student of John Dewey's and a major proponent of the Values Clarification model for moral education in America, defines values as "those elements that show how a person has decided to put his life right" (1966, 45). Raths means to suggest that what one values as morally good can be differentiated aesthetically. One pursues what one esteems, cherishes, finds endearing: that is, what puts life right. It is this fundamental differentiation that Robert Coles makes when he overcomes the puzzling ambiguities of Eduardo's moral character, when Coles finally comes to see "morality" as a matter of human possibilities, hopes, and aspirations rather than rules that prescribe certain behaviors and prohibit others. I have learned from Coles and Eduardo, then, an important lesson as a teacher concerned with students' moral lives and moral languages. There are wrong questions to ask of morality: for example, What are students' assumptions governing right and wrong? Where do those assumptions derive? Which rules or conventions do such assumptions either fulfill or violate? The right questions: What do students say about personal aspiration and hope? What self-images inform their moral discourses? How has the culture shaped, or maybe delimited, or perhaps deformed, images of personal being relative to the obligations the self has toward others? How do students struggle to put their lives right? Where has language either failed or fulfilled their moral struggles? Are students, as Nietzsche professed for humankind generally, "animals with red cheeks"? Or do they seek, as Cardinal Newman believed, "the repose of a mind which lives in itself, while it lives in the world"?

REFERENCES

Berlin, James. 1984. *Writing Instruction in Nineteenth-Century Colleges.* Carbondale: Southern Illinois University Press.

Booth, Wayne. 1988. *The Company We Keep: An Ethics of Fiction.* Berkeley: University of California Pres.

Botstein, Leon. 1990. "Damaged Literacy: Illiteracies and American Democracy." *Daedalus* 119.2: 55–84.

Coles, Robert. 1986. *The Moral Life of Children.* Boston: Houghton.

Damon, William. 1990. "Reconciling the Literacies of Generations." *Daedalus* 119.2: 33–53.

Goody, Jack. 1977. *The Domestication of the Savage Mind.* Cambridge: Cambridge University Press.

Kilpatrick, William. 1992. *Why Johnny Can't Tell Right from Wrong: Moral Illiteracy and the Case for Character Education.* New York: Simon and Schuster.

Kohlberg, Lawrence. 1976. "Moral Stages and Moralization: The Cognitive-Developmental Approach." *Moral Development and Moral Behavior.* Ed. Thomas Lickona. New York: Holt: 31–53.

Lanham, Richard. 1983. *Literacy and the Survival of Humanism.* New Haven: Yale University Press.

MacIntyre, Alasdair. 1984. *After Virtue: A Study in Moral Theory.* 2nd ed. South Bend, IN: University of Notre Dame Press.

Raths, Louis, Merrill Harmin, and Sidney B. Simon. 1966. *Values and Teaching: Working with Values in the Classroom.* Columbus, OH: Merrill.

Street, Brian. 1984. *Literacy in Theory and Practice.* New York: Cambridge University Press.

Tocqueville, Alexis de. 1945. *Democracy in America.* New York: A.A. Knopf.

Trilling, Lionel. 1979. *Liberal Imagination: Essays on Literature and Society.* New York: Harcourt.

Tuman, Myron. 1987. *A Preface to Literacy: An Inquiry into Pedagogy, Practice, and Progress.* Tuscaloosa: University of Alabama Press.

READING, WRITING, AND

REFLECTION (1998)

"WHAT REALLY IRKED ME ABOUT BETTY'S DECISION," RUDY WRITES in his journal, "was that it should have been an editorial decision based on layout, design balance, etc. Instead, it was based on a phony rationale. The incident had an adverse effect on my outlook towards service at the Center." Rudy explains:

> When Betty and I discussed the final edits for the newsletter, she also explained to me that there was to be a change in the layout. [U.S.] Senator [Spencer] Abraham would not have his picture included in his story [about renaissance zones in Michigan]. Another individual, Flint Mayor Woodrow Stanley, had just sent a photo of himself to accompany his article. Mayor Stanley happens to be Black. Since Newt Gingrich's photo was already running with his story [on the Earning by Learning program Gingrich founded for inner-city youngsters], it would be "more balanced" if we ran a photo of the Black gentleman and withheld Abraham's, providing an element of diversity. . . . I am simply tired of hearing we should/should not do something based on the color of a person's skin. This type of action does nothing to advance the fight against

discrimination. It is a way for those in charge to give the appearance of a diversified newsletter. . . . This one incident affected my outlook on the service I was doing.

As part of a required service-learning component for his general-education writing class, Rudy chose an assignment as newsletter assistant at his university's outreach office for community and economic development, where he works closely with Betty editing articles that appear in the center's monthly newsletter. The community placements chosen for students in Rudy's class were carefully selected as good sites for "real time" writing projects that address tangible and responsive audiences and link writing in a field of the student's choosing—in Rudy's case, public administration—with formal classroom-based writing activities and instruction. In addition to writing for an agency, students are required to keep a written journal record that functions both as further writing practice and, more important, as opportunities for students to reflect critically and systematically on their service experiences.

In his next journal entry Rudy relates an incident that has no ostensible bearing on diversity policy. At the prompting of his teacher, Rudy chooses instead to write about Betty herself, seeking some insight into her personality and the character of her commitment.

> As we were leaving the Center last Tuesday so that Betty could give me a ride home, the family that lives next door to the center arrived home. They were obviously an economically disadvantaged family, since they lived in a less affluent part of the city. As Betty was getting in the car, the little girl from next door called her name and came racing over. Immediately Betty gave the little girl a big hug, and asked about her day at school, etc. This scene may have had nothing to do with my work, and it may have been just a minor event in the grand scheme of things, but it touched me. Here was a woman that was so compassionate and caring, and here was a little girl who respected and appreciated this relationship so much. It really gave me a bit of insight into Betty's nature. It became clear why she was working at the center. She was inherently a person with

a great deal of love to give. That's simply a part of her make-up, and it was evidenced by this scene. One could tell that Betty truly believed that nothing, not even a poor economic situation, could hinder this young girl's future. And I think I felt the same.

Even though Rudy takes pains to point out that the scene in the driveway "may have had nothing to do with my [actual] work," it still has powerful resonance for his attitude toward service and the legitimacy of his service-learning assignment at the Center. Indirectly, even covertly, Rudy's discovery of the depth and authenticity of Betty's commitment to her work surely complicates, as his teacher may have hoped, that attitude of certainty he had earlier used to dismiss Betty's editorial decision as partisan, ideologically driven, and politically motivated.

STRUCTURING CRITICAL REFLECTION

The journals that Rudy and his classmates kept are modeled on the "critical incident journal" format devised by Timothy K. Stanton (1995). The "critical incident" technique differs from more traditional journal narratives in several ways. Primarily, Stanton explains as he addresses students directly, "rather than a descriptive record of daily life, a critical incident journal includes detailed analysis of only those incidents which change you or your perspective on your service experience. . . . Rather than simply describing and interpreting an incident and the people involved," Stanton continues, "this reflective technique enables [you] to use the incident and its impact as a means for self-monitoring and personal exploration" (59). In addition to identifying an event and describing its relevant details, the critical incident journal format requires students to pursue three rhetorical steps spanning *description*, *analysis*, and *reflection*.

STEP 1: Describe your role in the incident. What did you do? How did you react? How did others react?

35

STEP 2: Analyze the incident. How well or how poorly did you understand the situation? Was your reaction—or the reaction of others—well informed or based on misinformation? How did you handle it? What would you do differently next time?

STEP 3: What impact did the incident have on you? Why do you view it as "critical"? How has the incident influenced your feelings about working at your placement site? What have you learned? How has your perspective on yourself or others been changed and/or reinforced? Where do you go from here?

When responding to his first journal entry, Rudy's teacher notes that he describes the incident surrounding Betty's photo layout decision with precision and good detail, but his reaction to it, she suggests, may be more emotive—"What really irked me . . ."—than critically reflective. She encourages him, then, to either revisit the incident in another entry or select a new incident to write about with special attention to fleshing out Step 3. Rudy's teacher also wisely defers direct comment on Rudy's conclusion that the episode over the picture layout evidences a phony diversity policy. Nor does she broach the issue of Rudy's boilerplate conservatism, a political alignment he had proudly and skillfully underscored in earlier journal entries—as if itching to provoke her own liberalism. Instead, she focuses on the way Rudy bookends his journal entry with references to unarticulated attitude changes. She encourages Rudy to spell out the exact changes in his outlook toward service brought about by the incident. In an effort to redirect his antagonism, she also urges him again—an urging that prompts Rudy's follow-up entry—to write about another incident at the Center that either confirms or perhaps confounds his strong belief that Betty's editorial decision grew out of a bogus rationale for racial diversity.

With the help of the critical incident format, Rudy's teacher provides, in short, new conditions and ramifications that seek to redirect Rudy's natural powers of curiosity into investigations that are more intellectually responsible and more critically engaged. In doing so, she seizes on the rival interpretations that open Rudy's first passage to critical scrutiny—what progressive educational theorist and public philosopher John Dewey called "the strife of alternative interpretations" (1933, 121). It may not be enough, she suggests, to be "simply tired of hearing" about racial diversity. She persists in posing questions that push Rudy to think in new ways, to reflect critically, and to question his own perceptions of what he considers a critical incident at the Center. Why, for example, should one choose pictures for a newsletter based on typographic considerations alone? Do race-based editorial decisions over layout send important and defensible messages to readers in support of diversity? Which of these competing interpretations has the rightful claim? And what implications, she hints, might that "rightful claim" have for Betty's integrity?

TRANSFORMING VALUES THROUGH REFLECTION

The narrative development between Rudy's two journal entries—from static indignation to dynamic reaffirmation, from annoyance to rectitude—captures, in fact, what John Dewey considered as the primary function of reflective thought: "to transform a situation in which there is experienced . . . conflict [or] disturbance of some sort, into a situation that is clear, coherent, settled, harmonious. . . . Genuine thinking winds up, in short, with an appreciation of new values" (1933, 100–101). It is important to point out that Rudy continues to write favorably about articles and opinions advancing the conservative agenda. "The key to turning around the urban disadvantaged," he later writes, "lies in programs that promote rugged individualism, rather than encouraging people to expect a handout." His curiosity and powers of inquiry shift, however, to the moral integrity of those who act on behalf of policy and away from the validity or political viability of the policies themselves. Rudy's political conservatism begins to expand and take on a communitarian ring—once again illustrating Dewey's belief that "all reflective thinking is a process of detecting relations. . . ." (1933, 77). For example, Rudy writes about how "one can show their compassion by forming ideas . . . such as people help themselves," and how urban renewal policies must "provide a greater good: helping the community as a whole." His new interests in moral consensus and the common good, moreover, reveal the kinds of social attitudes that naturally grow out of reflective thought and, Dewey further believed, are indispensable to the nurture of democracy and responsible citizenship. "The clear consciousness of a communal life, in all its implications," according to Dewey, "constitutes the idea of democracy" (Robertson 1992, 341). That clarifying consciousness can be seen in Rudy's willingness to reevaluate his beliefs in light of Betty's different attitude about photo layout and diversity, Rudy's reconsideration of public policy in terms of the community as a whole, and ultimately—what he may have been most "touched by" when the child raced over to embrace Betty—his realization that one's own good cannot be easily separated from the good of others.

In many respects, Rudy's experience at the Center encapsulates a tension among service-learning educators and practitioners that is best resolved through the use of structured critical reflection exercises and techniques like the critical incident journal. Should Rudy's teacher, to put it bluntly, set out to redirect, indeed redress, his political and social conservatism? Or is Rudy's social consciousness incidental to the academic work going on at the intersection of his assignment at the Center and his enrollment in a writing class at his university? What is the proper character, in other words, of her intervention? Should the goal of a service-learning-infused curriculum be the preparation of students like Rudy for social action skills? Or intellectual competence and working knowledge in service of students' courses of academic study? To track Rudy's learning curve along separate social and cognitive spectra may beg, however, the wrong questions. In point of fact, Rudy's case may suggest that solving social problems vis-à-vis active community involvement and engaging intellectual processes may be more complementary than polarized. Rudy simultaneously learns to apply critical intelligence to his political beliefs while he engages in a practice of building democratic awareness and democratic community at the Center. He submits his political beliefs to the stimulus of critical reflection, not to a political litmus. He learns to formulate new questions about old habits of thought. He learns the important difference between an *opinion* passionately felt and powerfully held and a *problem* that needs to be solved and for which answers must be sought. He undergoes what David Kolb describes as "learning [that] transforms . . . impulses, feelings, and desires . . . into higher-order purposeful action" (1984, 22). If anything, ideology loses its exclusive and unchallenged grip on Rudy's political conservatism. His passion for rugged individualism now carries an ethical valence that transforms it into a more socially responsive conservatism: a conservatism, it could be said, with an articulate moral philosophy.

In the development of his narrative reflections, Rudy discovers that a valuation he previously held no longer works well for him. He could no longer satisfactorily dismiss Betty's editorial decision as politically motivated and, as such, rooted shallowly in ideological ground. He begins instead to experiment with alternative modes of valuation based on ethical and moral criteria and then to experimentally test those criteria to find out whether a *life*, as well as social policy, can be guided more satisfactorily according to them. Rudy is clearly more moved by the Betty who elicits the child's tender affections than he is by the Betty who makes an editorial decision based on racial balance.

Moreover, not only does Rudy's service experience at the Center provide a real situation that arouses his powers of inquiry and insight, but he encounters in Betty someone who, quite simply and directly, thinks and acts differently. Given his teacher's encouragement to rethink his beliefs through the encounter with someone who believes differently, Rudy learns more about diversity—its complexity, its interpersonal ramifications, its socioethical consequences, its rootedness in the common good—than he could have in weeks of reading and classroom discussion alone.

EXPERIENTIAL ROOTS OF REFLECTIVE THINKING

In a word, Rudy undergoes what several generations of modern educational theorists—beginning with John Dewey and cresting in the more recent work of David Kolb—refer to formally as an *experiential learning cycle* that

39

is driven, in large part, by the adaptive learning modality of *reflective observation*. Arguing for the reflexive nature of learning processes, David Kolb (1984) acknowledges the dynamic spiral character of knowledge formation and its anchorage in a student's concrete, lived experience. "Ideas are not fixed and immutable elements of thought," he explains, "but are formed and re-formed through experience. . . . [L]earning is . . . a process whereby concepts are derived from and continuously modified by experience" (26). Rudy's service-learning assignment at the Center provides a good case, in fact, for what Dewey and Kolb view as the "situatedness of reflective thinking" (Dewey 1933, 99) that is both the indispensable agent, Dewey argues, and the object of knowledge formation. Follow the thread of an idea or "the stuff of knowledge far enough," Dewey writes, "and you will find some situation that is directly experienced, something undergone, done, enjoyed, or suffered, and not just thought of. Reflection is occasioned by the character of this primary situation. It does not merely *grow out of it*," Dewey further maintains, "but it *refers back* to [the concrete learning situation]. [The] aims and outcomes [of reflective thinking] are decided by the situation out of which it arose" (1933, 99).

Reflective thinking is not only, then, an organic component in the learning cycle, it is simultaneously the very ground from which knowledge and belief spring. Reflective thinking, in short, is both process and product. As such, reflective thinking has become a key subject in the massive literature of experiential learning theory and, more recently, the operational linchpin of contemporary service-learning pedagogy (see, for example, Boud, Keogh, and Walker 1984; King and Kitchener 1994; Silcox 1993). At the same time, the centrality of reflective thinking has shaped the core arguments for service learning's ongoing critique of conventional classroom-based learning practices. "Probably the most frequent cause of failure in school to secure genuine thinking from students," as Dewey frames that critique, "is the failure to insure the existence of an experienced situation of such a nature as to call out [reflective] thinking in the way in which . . . out-of-school situations do" (1933, 99).

THEORETICAL FOUNDATIONS OF REFLECTIVE THINKING

In *How We Think*, John Dewey presents one of the most durable cases, as David Kolb acknowledges in the acclaimed *Experiential Learning* (1984), for the critical primacy of structured reflective thinking in the educative process. Together with other significant works—notably, *Experience and Education* (1938) and *Democracy and Education* (1916)—Dewey left an intellectual legacy that best articulates that process through the guiding principles of experiential learning, including the cultivation and expression of a student's individuality; the transformation of the classroom into a venue for free and independent activity, inquiry, and thought; and the importance of learning through experience. Growing out of his abiding faith in the scientific method and experimentalism and his deep dedication to radical democracy as the model for progressive education—the two central strands of Dewey's social and political philosophy—Dewey argues that reflective thinking is both the means and end that education, properly considered, ought to cultivate.

Dewey defines reflective thinking succinctly as "*active, persistent and careful consideration of any belief or supposed form of knowledge in the light of the grounds that support it and the further conclusions to which it tends*" (1933, 9). Extending his definition into the sphere of pedagogical practice, Dewey argues that reflective thought results from "careful and extensive study, . . . purposeful widening of the area of observation [under study], . . . [and] reasoning out the conclusions of alternative conceptions to see what would follow in case one or the other were adopted for belief" (1933, 8). For Dewey, reflective thinking is essential to the pragmatic application of the scientific attitude and outlook to human life and education. It therefore encompasses *cognitive processes* such as the logical management of an orderly chain of ideas to a controlling purpose and end, *social or democratic functions* called upon when public conflicts demand resolution through common problem-solving and effective public discourse, and the *ethical skills* that Dewey adopts as the attitude ground of reflective thinking: open-mindedness, whole-heartedness, and intellectual responsibility.

Addressing the values that reflective thinking instills, Dewey writes:

> Reflective thought . . . emancipates us from merely impulsive and merely
> routine activity. . . . [Reflective] thinking enables us to direct our activi-
> ties with foresight and to plan according to ends-in-view, or purposes
> of which we are aware. It enables us to act in deliberate and intentional
> fashion. . . . [I]t enables us to *know what we are about* when we act. *It*
> *converts action that is merely appetitive, blind, and impulsive into intelligent*
> *action.*" (1933, 17)

Reflective thinking is always inaugurated by what Dewey calls a "forked-
road" situation in which a student faces an ambiguous dilemma that
confronts him or her with the reliability and the worth of a previously held
belief. "Difficulty or obstruction," Dewey continues, "in the way of reach-
ing a belief brings us . . . to a pause. In the suspense of uncertainty[,] . . .
demand for the solution of a perplexity is the steadying and guiding factor
in the entire process of reflection" (1933, 14). David Kolb synthesizes Dewey's point into one of the central premises of current experiential learning
theory. "The process of learning," Kolb (1984) states, "requires the resolution of conflicts between dialectically opposed modes of adaptation to the
world" (29). Kolb is quick to add that "reflective observation abilities" are
indispensable agents in that experience of adaptation.

Dewey takes pains to break that process of engaging a dilemma down
into multiple aspects or "terminals" of reflective activity that span three progressive stages: problematization, hypothesis formation, and testing of the
hypothesis. "Reflective thinking," Dewey summarizes, "involves (1) a state
of doubt, hesitation, perplexity, mental difficulty, in which thinking originates, and (2) an act of searching, hunting, inquiring, to find material that
will resolve the doubt, settle and dispose of the perplexity" (1933, 12). The
movement from doubt to the disposition of a perplexity is engendered, first
and foremost, by what Dewey insists are the critical conditions under which
students must work and learn: "the provision of a real situation that arouses
inquiry, suggestion, reasoning, testing, etc." (283). This emphasis on the situatedness of reflective observation and its centrality to the learning process

leads to a statement of David Kolb's that has become a widely quoted catch-phrase of the contemporary experiential learning movement: *"Learning is the process whereby knowledge is created through the transformation of experience"* (1984, 38).

PRACTICING CRITICAL REFLECTION

Among the many successful efforts to render John Dewey's and David Kolb's theories of reflective thinking into practical classroom application, Janet Eyler, Dwight Giles, and Angela Schmiede's *A Practitioner's Guide to Reflection in Service-Learning* (1996) stands out as particularly illuminating and incisive. Not only do Eyler, Giles, and Schmiede succeed in putting theory into practice, but, more important, their guide to reflection activities and techniques grows out of hundreds of structured interviews with students across the country enrolled in service-learning courses. This student-centered approach lends a considerable degree of legitimacy to the Vanderbilt University team's investigations of service-learning practices and the strategies they propose to achieve successful critical reflection for students and teachers in service-based courses across the disciplines. Those strategies range from reading, writing, and oral exercises to project-based activities and collaborative action research. "The experiences of the students we encountered through this study," the authors write, "[emphasize] . . . that reflection is the glue that holds service and learning together to provide [optimal] educative experiences" (16).

The authors' research indicates that there are four principal criteria for successful application of reflective thinking to students' service-learning experiences. They compress these criteria into "the 4 Cs of reflection." "Over the course of this study," they conclude, "certain themes have reappeared repeatedly as critical factors in effective reflective activity. The best reflection is *Continuous* in time frame, *Connected* to the 'big picture' information provided by academic pursuits, *Challenging* to assumptions and complacency, and *Contextualized* in terms of design and setting" (21).

In using their interview data to structure reflection guidelines, Eyler, Giles, and Schmiede stress that reflection activities must flex according to various student learning styles. After all, students "learn to learn" in different ways. Therefore, service-learning faculty and coordinators should ideally offer a variety of reflection activities that accommodate differences across the range of student learning styles that Eyler, Giles, and Schmiede identify as "activists," "reflectors," "theorists," and "pragmatists." In addition, the authors offer a "Reflection Activity Matrix" that reminds service-minded educators just how integral critical reflection is to other learning activities and modalities. Reflective thinking is not a mere supplement to conventional learning techniques. It is an integral component in a process that fuses reading, writing, doing, telling, and reflecting into a learning ecology.

FROM EXPECTATION TO EXPERIENCE

As service-learning practitioners themselves, Eyler, Giles, and Schmiede realize that the most important element in effective reflection is also the most difficult and problematic for teachers to implement successfully: the challenge of pushing students to think critically and to engage issues in a more critically reflective way. Challenging reflection involves a hard balancing act. A teacher must be willing to intervene, pose tough questions, and propose often uncomfortable points of view for a student's consideration. A teacher must also be ready to back off and give support in order to nurture the independence and autonomy that are the lifeblood of experiential learning processes. Revisiting Rudy's service-learning experience may suggest that achieving this balance is not strictly a matter of adopting frameworks and guidelines or following rules, but it is more a question of taking what service-learning practitioners recognize as the path to critical learning: "Learning is best conceived as a process . . . grounded in experience, not in terms of outcomes," as David Kolb puts it, and "a process . . . continuously modified by experience" (26–27). In other words, a good teacher is prepared to set his or her students upon a journey to knowledge, and then be willing to go along for the ride.

Returning to Rudy's service-learning assignment at the Center, much to his own credit he sets out to inquire into the meaning of what he learns and what difference it may have to his conservative beliefs. That search for meaning begins in Dewey's "forked-road" situation and it follows, as predicted by Kolb, a trajectory of transformation. On the one hand, Betty's editorial decision demonstrates, to Rudy's mind initially, that diversity is only a matter of "appearances." Therefore, he is inclined to dismiss Betty's actions as arbitrary. But given the interpersonal realities Rudy faces in his actual working relationship at the Center—the fact that his learning process is situated and grounded in lived experience—does it follow, as logically perhaps it must, that *Betty is an arbitrary person?* Should he not respect her?

Rudy's teacher occasions the ambiguity by inviting Rudy to probe into the implications Betty's layout decision has for changes in his attitudes about working at the Center. He must squarely face the antagonism he writes about in his journal over this incident against the great enthusiasm he has when returning to work at the Center—for Rudy continues to speak about how "stimulating" his service has been and how he is "gaining a better understanding of the nuts and bolts of editing a newsletter . . . while also looking at Michigan's distressed communities and ways to revitalize them." Rudy's teacher also positions Rudy in such a way that he has to confront and work through some unstated assumptions he might be making. Is Betty an enforcer of orthodoxy? And what about the mayor of Flint? Were it not for the color of his skin, does he *deserve* his picture on the newsletter cover? Paraphrasing Dewey, Rudy's teacher seizes on the real possibilities the incident harbors for Rudy to examine his assumptions more carefully and extensively, to widen the area of his inquiry into a cherished belief, and to follow his reasoning all the way out to conclusions and alternatives he had not before considered due to the narrow depth-of-field compassed by his initial dismissal of Betty's decision as biased and unfair. Rudy's teacher *problematizes* his strongly held belief that diversity is a matter of "appearances" alone and "does nothing to advance the fight against discrimination." She provides impetus to Rudy's formation of a hypothesis concerning whether

Betty's diversity policy is only skin-deep. And Rudy tests the hypothesis. He probes into the reliability of a belief that once seemed so indisputable and obvious, and he finds it wanting in light of his discovery of Betty's real passion for community.

Rudy's learning occurs right at the place David Kolb (1984) describes as "the interplay between expectation and experience," an interplay mediated by reflective thinking. John Dewey reminds us that, like Rudy, we all have

> the tendency to believe that which is in harmony with desire. We take that to be true which we should like to have so, and ideas that go contrary to our hopes and wishes have difficulty in getting lodgment. We jump to conclusions; we all fail to examine and test our ideas because of our personal attitudes. When we generalize, we tend to make sweeping assertions; that is, from one or only a few facts we make a generalization covering a wide field. Observation also reveals the powerful influence wielded by social influences that have actually nothing to do with the truth or falsity of what is asserted and denied. (1933, 28)

Education can help us reflect these tendencies, David Kolb wisely concludes: "If the education process begins by bringing out the learner's beliefs and theories, examining them and testing them, and then integrating the new, more refined ideas into the person's belief systems, the learning process," as in Rudy's case, "will be facilitated" (27).

REFERENCES

Boud, D., R. Keogh, and D. Walker, eds. 1984. *Reflection: Turning Experience into Learning*. New York: Routledge.

Dewey, J. 1916. *Democracy and Education*. New York: Free Press.

———. 1933. *How We Think*. New York: Heath.

———. 1938. *Experience and Education*. New York: Collier.

Eyler, J., Giles, D., and Schmiede, A. 1996. *A Practitioner's Guide to Reflection in Service-Learning: Student Voices and Reflections.* Nashville, TN: Vanderbilt University.

King, P. M., and K. S. Kitchener. 1994. *Developing Reflective Judgment: Understanding and Promoting Intellectual Growth and Critical Thinking in Adolescents and Adults.* San Francisco: Jossey-Bass.

Kolb, D. 1984. *Experiential Learning: Experience as the Source of Learning and Development.* Englewood Cliffs, NJ: Prentice-Hall.

Robertson, E. 1992. "Is Dewey's Educational Vision Still Viable?" *Review of Research in Education* 18: 335–381.

Silcox, H. C. 1993. *A How-To Guide to Reflection: Adding Cognitive Learning to Community Service Programs.* Philadelphia: Brighton Press.

Stanton, T. K. 1995. "Writing about Public Service: The Critical Incident Journal." *Guide for Change: Resources for Implementing Community Service Writing.* Ed. M. Ford and A. Watters. New York: McGraw-Hill.

THE CHANGING SEASONS OF

LIBERAL LEARNING (1998)

IN THE SPRING OF 1990, SEVERAL STUDENT GROUPS AT MY CAMPUS
erected shanties on a newly reclaimed "People's Park." Growing out of a
protest symbolism spurred by the antiapartheid and endowment divestiture
movements that briefly flourished on college campuses nationwide during
the mid-1980s, the People's Park shanties were aimed initially at heighten-
ing awareness of various social justice issues after a long winter of Big Ten
basketball and political hibernation.

The first five shanties were united into a community "Shantytown" by
a common protest discourse and shared political alignments. The groups
included HURT (Helping to Understand Racism Today). The Democratic
Socialists of America set up a shanty protesting homelessness in America and
promoting an alternative social vision of what its members felt was fairer
economic justice. Another shanty, organized by the student Committee for
Education on Latin America (CELA), stood as a memorial to the late Salva-
dorian archbishop and martyred social democrat Oscar Romero. Sponsored
by the local chapter of Take Back the Night and a proactive environmental
group, the remaining two shanties advanced this theme of political dissent
and consciousness-raising linked to underclass empowerment.

THE ANTI-SHANTY SHANTY

The first counterprotest shanty appeared barely two weeks after People's Park was reclaimed as the protest turf of liberal student organizations. Built by CASH (Conservative Anti-Shanty Haters), the antishanty shanty differed as much in visual appearance as in political alignment from those erected earlier. Instead of a jury-rigged A-frame, CASH's shanty was scaled along lines of a conventional suburban ranch, looking like something out of a home improvement TV show. It was painted white. The window frames and fascia were neatly trimmed in the school colors, Spartan Green. Plastic geraniums sprouted from window flower boxes flanking the front door. A white picket fence ran the perimeter of the shanty's mock front yard. Tidy stepping stones led from the gate to a front door welcome mat. The *Wall Street Journal* was cradled in a mailbox that bore a street number—1899—and a nicely painted fleur-de-lis. On the roof, the initials "CASH" and "POLO" were carefully lettered in the block style of the famous Spartan "S." (The latter acronym, like a gap-toothed word puzzle on the popular TV quiz show *Wheel of Fortune*, was the subject of much speculation in the student newspaper.) Two plastic chaise lounges graced the front yard, one garnished tastefully by another edition of the *Wall Street Journal* opened to the stock tables. The CASH architects placed a placard on the front lawn that carried the antishanty shanty's visual imagery into verbal territory. Pro-corporate anti-rain forest pro-deforestation slogans were bolstered by antiliberal sentiment clothed in the popular cant of ardent nationalism, including "Cry Me a River: The American Way of Life is the Only Way" and "Support Your Constitution and Your Flag." More bellicose reminders of CASH's social agenda: "Scum: Go Back to Where You Belong" (an apparent allusion to CELA's memorial to Oscar Romero) and a swipe at the feminist orientation of Take Back the Nighters, "Put the 'e' back in Womyn." An anti-affirmative action slogan directed against HURT elicited a comment, lifted from the title of a new, in-your-face album release from the hip-hop group Public Enemy, spray-painted on the sidewalk in front of CASH's gate: "Fear of a

Black Planet!" That graffiti, in turn, drew an irate response in a letter to the student newspaper from a "sophomore computer science major" who complained about vandalism to the university's sidewalks. "People's Park is ugly enough," he protested. "Must we make the ugliness permanent?"

Other antishanty shanties quickly proliferated. The organizer of SALT (Students Against Liberal Trash) was quoted in the campus newspaper as saying, "I am willing to be publicly viewed as an idiot just to get people thinking and also to heighten their awareness about issues." His martyrdom, his efforts at consciousness-raising, and his calculation of personal IQ inspired the following hieroglyphics inscribed on SALT's own antishanty shanty: "Affirmative Action Sucks," "Get Help Gays," and "Minority in a Minute" with an arrow pointing to a bucket of black paint.

The countercurrent of conservative student animus stirred by CASH and SALT soon unleashed a nastier undercurrent of intolerance from anonymous quarters of the student body. A final antishanty shanty was surreptitiously constructed one night, and the next morning People's Park was greeted by the following comments:

"White Niggers Go Too!"

"Fuck Affirmative Action. Let Them Work Like We Do"

"5,000,000 Wasn't Enough" (This statistic, I can only imagine, was an anti-Semitic allusion to the six million Jews who perished in the Holocaust. But who's keeping count? Hard-working students don't have time to track down *every* statistic.)

"We Can't Have Queers Protecting Our Country or Flag"

"I'm Not Racist. But I Keep My Genes Clean"

"If You Are Looking for Problems in America, Check the Jew and Nigger Community"

The campus administration, citing antiobscenity regulations, moved quickly (and properly) to dismantle the last shanty erected before the entire issue of the People's Park revival languished into summer vacation, and then completely disappeared.

MOLOCH AND THE MATERIAL GIRL

Today's neoconservative, indeed reactionary campus outfits like CASH and SALT reveal the stark changes that have swept over college campuses, like a great social tsunami, in the past twenty years or so. For those undergraduates of my generation who rode out the campus storms of the late sixties and early seventies, who entered academic life in a flush of intellectual vitality leavened by social idealism, who hunkered down and (barely) survived the prolonged (and continuing) famine of the academic job market that began in the mid-seventies, who managed somehow to stay awake (and employed, even if marginally) during the eighties when the intellectual climate in arts and humanities was dominated by ponderous, narcoleptic theoretical abstractions, and who now find themselves—politically ambivalent, ideologically winded, intellectually adrift, publicly excoriated—on the doormat of what promises to be a new era of fiscal retrenchment and metaphysical revolution, the past couple decades seem like nothing less than a complete flip-flop in the moral tonality—the "feel"—that defines the life of institutions of higher education. The political cartoonist Gary Trudeau captured something of that kaleidoscopic shift in consciousness and mood when, in one of his last panels before taking an extended vacation from the op-ed pages, he had Mike Doonesbury, a consummate baby boomer, grasp his head—partly in confusion, partly in recognition, partly in desperation—and declare, "I have become my parents!" For those 1970s Ph.D.s whom *The Chronicle of Higher Education* (May 23, 1990) labeled collectively as "the lost generation," I wonder: Have students become our parents too?

Linear metaphors that measure progress, growth, transformation, and synthesis are inadequate to describe the changes that are the ballast to Doonesbury's epiphany. Metaphors of transmutation or antithesis—like the uroboros, the symbol of a snake swallowing its tail, or, more simply, of a sock being turned inside out—seem more appropriate and accurate. One wonders if the vapid material determinism, the ethical relativism, and the moral self-enclosure of today's college students are transmutations of the iconoclastic mysticism that animated—powerfully, if only briefly—my generation and scribed its ideological trajectory: the return of the hipster in a three-piece suit. Can we reach back into the sixties and grasp tightly to idealism and communitarianism—"Ask not what your country can do for you but what *you* can do for your country"—and pull forward through two decades to find them transmuted into an antithetical fatalism, acquisitive individualism, uncritical conformism? "Ask not what you can do for your country, but what's in it for me." Has Allen Ginsberg become Madonna?

A LETTER TO THE NEXT GENERATION

Such transmutations look entirely different, however, from the vantage point of a present generation struggling to emerge into self-definition from the ominous shadow cast by a previous generation whose rebelliousness must feel almost like a ritual obligation to today's students. Imagine what a legacy of social activism feels like to today's understandably cynical under-graduates who have learned a sour lesson about the possibilities for social change from their own generation's defining historical moments, from gas lines, Watergate and a hostage crisis to Iran-Contra, the S & L fiasco, and the House banking scandal known as Rubbergate. Sometimes it seems as if the only viable alternative for them is self-enclosure, withdrawal from the social arena altogether, or a retreat into privacy, nihilism, or the tenuous rewards of careerism.

Raised on TV culture where reality comes at them through the web-less seam of television news, today's students are drawn into, according to Neil Postman in *Amusing Ourselves to Death* (1985), "an epistemology based on the assumption that all reports of cruelty and death are [transient and] greatly exaggerated and, in any case, not to be taken seriously or responded to sanely" (105). Pessimism about the future is reinforced by a pervasive historical pessimism among many adults to whom the past looks no better than the future. Historical pessimism is especially heightened—indeed *warranted*—as the current generation views the past from the vantage point of a present where debate rages over the deterioration of values, the loss of ethical standards in business, and the general decline of civility in America suggested by the popular slogans of a president imagining a kinder, gentler nation during a decade of governmental gridlock, record-breaking murder and suicide rates, and bracket creep among statistics that track violent crime. Not to mention the terribly confusing signals sent by an advertising industry intent on linking the empowerment of women and minorities to consumerism and the cult of celebrity, and the equally confusing signals sent by pundits like Rush Limbaugh and Maxine Waters, who argue over differences between riots and insurrections while America's inner cities seethe with resentment and despair. Consider too the unprecedented hammering of Generation X starting with *Nation at Risk* (1983), continuing unabated throughout the eighties, buttressed by a high-brow caning handed out by Allan Bloom in his 1987 best seller *The Closing of the American Mind,* and tracked with great precision by Alexander Austin and the Higher Education Research Institute at UCLA, whose annual logarithms suggest that each year's high school graduation class appears generally stupider and more socially disengaged than the previous year's. Is it any wonder Leon Botstein, writing in a special issue of *Daedalus* in 1990, reluctantly concludes that "a sense of decline, deterioration, and futility hangs over the American classroom"?

Few young persons have managed as clean a breakthrough as twenty-something writer Arion Berger, who has come to feel "less need to borrow identities" from the omnipresent earth-rattling sixties culture, "less fear that I'll wake up and be someone I did not create and cannot change," she writes in a clutch of letters received by filmmaker Jim Klein in response to his film *Letter to the Next Generation.* "I've learned that underneath the fakery I've rented," she continues, "there's something that's mine alone." For most people Ms. Berger's age, however, there are other lessons to be learned from the cultural fault lines that separate college students today from the baby boomer professoriate just now rising to demographic—and political—prominence on campus. Perhaps more to the point is the confused animosity felt by a senior at Cornell University sparked by forty-three-year-old Jim Klein's film. The student fired off a letter of his own to Klein (and *his* generation) immediately after the film first aired on public television in July 1990. While in many ways moved by the film's challenges to his generation, the student's letter eventually turns to the intergenerational anxieties of influence that are too often unacknowledged irritants in faculty/student relations today. "I do hate to say it," the senior letter-writer admits, but "many in my generation resent the generation before—the Baby Boomers."

> Many young people [today] see the Boomers as a generation that grew up in the Levittowns with no cares, went to college as a matter of course and denounced the wealth they always knew their families could give them in a bind, played activist for a while and became investment bankers whey they got tired of it, while continually stopping on the way to dump tons of garbage on Woodstock, develop a sexist-as-hell hippie culture, and generally chew up the world and spit it out as they saw fit. Baby Boomers still have news reports about them, have a special edition of Trivial Pursuit just for them, have a Top 40 pop song (Billy Joel's "We Didn't Start the Fire") about the span of their lives and how they really are absolved of all responsibility for all that's happened, etc., etc., etc., etc. Who in our ignored generation *wouldn't* feel irritated, angered, and insecure enough to just want to buy all the dinosaurs out and shut them up once and for all? Or so goes the diatribe of many of my contemporaries, and yes, I sympathize, and even share some of the sentiments. . . . It's what happens when you are part of a generation without a name, overshadowed by another generation that refuses to fade away.

There is plenty in the film that justifies, although may not completely warrant, the letter-writer's own diatribe, for in fairness to Klein his film—which chronicles a return to Kent State University twenty years after the infamous May 4 killings of four students by National Guardsmen during an antiwar rally—is as introspectively questioning of his own generation as it is bluntly critical of contemporary Kent State students with their ball caps on backwards, singing "The Brady Bunch," theme song for Generation X. Part of the film's strength is its parallel avenues of critical insight into both a past generation's difficulty in letting go of its postadolescent iconoclasm and its indefatigable mystique of nonconformity, and a present generation's cynical detachment from social concerns and its desperate search for ways to fit in—insights at loggerhead in the film until mediated by a charge to the "Next Generation" to step meaningfully into the breach.

But the film is mostly about intergenerational antagonism, about two generations uneasily eyeing each other from across a values divide that seems, at times, unbridgeable, without a common language or a binding history, without a shared moral discourse that might otherwise fill the awkward moments when fortysomething faculty (and filmmakers) and students stare blankly, even smugly, at each other, the dialogue silenced by faculty disillusionment on one side and eyerolling student skepticism on the other.

The film is loaded with imagery that, frankly, indulges the stock values stereotypes often exploited by mass media (e.g., *Time* magazine's July 16, 1990, cover story on twentysomething angst) to market the Thirteenth Generation's crisis of disbelief. Those stereotypes include the ubiquitous (and ironic) dualism that pits what one student calls "the regular world" against the fast-food corporate wonderland of campus life; the self-enclosure, vanity, apathy, and cynicism routinely ascribed to today's college students, along with their disconnection from history, their obsessive career orientation and penchant for resume-building; the prevalence of the corporate paradigm at Kent State with its ethic of efficiency, cost-effectiveness, style-brand recognition, teamwork, professionalism, productivity, regulated consumption, and its clearly demarcated lines of decision-making, authority, reward; and, not the least, the majority of Kent students' insensitivity to and general unconcern for issues of race/class/gender pressed unrelentingly by the campus Left. As on most campuses, that latter trend is countervailed at Kent State by a small minority of students whose commitments to wider social concerns put to rout the charge of pervasive self-interest and political disengagement too often leveled at college students today by disaffected baby boomers. It was this juxtaposition of conflicting commitments that prompted another college senior to write Klein barely two hours after the film aired. "Your mixture of the negatives and positives that exist in the reality of our generation," she said, "touched hard. The way you looked at the events that shaped (and are still shaping) our generation into a primarily capitalistic and financial-success oriented society were so understandable. . . . Your film is an inspiration to those of us who *see*," she concluded, "as well as those who have yet to."

Letter to the Next Generation is full of more treatments of intergenerational friction than can be explored in much detail here. But there are three episodes that might serve as a vivid backdrop to the discussion that follows, maybe part of the sociomoral scenery that Gary Trudeau had in mind when he staged Mike Doonesbury's initiation into nineties adulthood and his sudden realization of what it's really like growing up absurd.

In the first scene, Klein takes his camera into Kent's Electric Beach, a tanning salon on the campus perimeters where, we are told, about a hundred students a day work on their tans. A student lies on a tanning bed that looks like a cross between a neon clamshell and an iron lung. She is wearing a bikini and eyecups.

FEMALE ON TANNING BED: I just really enjoy the tan and I enjoy having color in my skin. It makes me feel a lot better about myself and it's also a lot healthier looking. . . .

FILMMAKER TO TANNING GUYS: What types of women do you like?

TANNING GUYS: Tan. Definitely tan. . . .

I could pass a tan for other things.

If she doesn't have a tan . . . We'll get her a tan.

That's a big question. What do we like them for? I mean, like them to keep. Two or three years from now I'll be looking for a wife, look for a nice little homebody to settle down with but right now it's hot . . . definitely hot. . . .

FEMALE ON TANNING BED: Well, I like to keep myself in shape and I like to look great and I like to exercise.

Later, Klein visits a class session for a sociology course on Utopian Societies. The professor first came to Kent State in 1967. While teaching sociology, he also took part in demonstrations against the Vietnam War and was indicted for incitement to riot after the May 4 shootings.

PROFESSOR AT THE BLACKBOARD: The idea is to reward everyone at least similarly. . . . Regardless of ability. Don't reward ability.

STUDENT: If you don't reward ability you won't have any incentive . . . why would a doctor want to be a doctor? or a lawyer be a lawyer when we're all going to get the same amount of money?

STUDENT: Chances are a lot of people who would be doctors and be good doctors won't become doctors.

PROFESSOR IN FRONT OF CLASS: . . . if you're doing something that is rather interesting and being a medical doctor is probably pretty interesting—I know being a Ph.D. is interesting. Then that's kind of its own reward. If you think of yourself as having to measure up to standards, you're playing their game by their rules, you have to take the system as given and you never will try to change it. You'll just try to make yourself comfortable within it. This is what the professional does. This is what I do. I make myself comfortable within a rotten system and I get off the hook by telling others that we should all ban together and change this as best we can.

(Students take notes.)

After class, Klein asks the sociology professor what kinds of questions his students ask. "Not many," he replies.

Near the end of the film, Klein interviews a student in his dorm room. He comments on a poster taped to the wall, a sumptuous photograph of two sports cars flanked by a phrase printed elegantly along the top.

STUDENT: I thought it was kind of unique, you know. That little saying up top, you know, "The Rewards of a Higher Education" . . . you make it through this is what you're going to get, you know . . . My mama bought that for me for a Christmas gift. . . .

FILMMAKER: What do you see your goal coming out of college to be?

STUDENT: Wow, like goals is like materials or like within me?

FILMMAKER: Whatever. . . .

STUDENT: Getting a good job. . . . Feel like I had done something, you know, for the corporation.

FILMMAKER: You know what I see missing? The thing I'm really interested that you don't say is that . . . what would make you feel a success . . . if you had really helped change somebody's life . . . or made a difference say in the society or like that . . . do you ever think about that?

STUDENT: Like helping someone out . . . like philantropic [*sic*] like that way, you know?. . . . No, I've never really thought about helping my fellow man if that's what you're bringing up, which is I can see what you're getting at. . . . That is missing I think definitely from the college student of the eighties.

TRANSMUTATIONS

During the free speech and antiwar movements of the sixties, some faculty members, like Richard Sewall, a professor of literature at Yale, misread the dramatic upheavals on college campuses as a new millennialism, "a coming of age," he put it then in a memo to the university president urging a conciliatory tone with campus activists, "on the part of students, a putting away of the trivia inherited from the past [and] a real desire to enter into and share the true spirit of the University community" (Smith 1990, 162). Peter Clecak, a historian at the University of California, Irvine (which, during the mid-sixties, not incidentally, was gearing up a building program to fulfill Clark Kerr's vision of the "true spirit" of the new American "multiversity"), correctly assessed the connection between student unrest over the Vietnam War and the numbing bureaucratization of academic life. In his 1983 book *America's Quest for the Ideal Self: Dissent and Fulfillment in the 60s and 70s*, Clecak wrote sympathetically of students who complained vociferously about "a lack of 'identity' and an absence of 'community'" on college campuses. Student agitation, he reckoned, derived from an encounter with "the institution or the 'system' [as] confusing, impersonal, and depersonalizing." Students resent, he noted, "those of us [on the faculty] who fail to develop—or even to seek—a style adequate to what we profess and adequate to the students' need for admirable and imitable adults. In short, they find the faculty morally corrupt, emotionally stunted and intellectually sterile—irrelevant . . . to their lives" (47).

The same charges stick today. Except, like role models and generational heroes—Clecak's "imitable adults"—the charges have to be turned inside out. Paraphrasing Sewell, faculty today are likely to view *students* as thriving on conventions and trivia inherited from the past and possessing, at best, a reluctance, at worst, a repugnance to enter into and share in the "true spirit" of a university community. Faculty today are more inclined to deride *students* for what students twenty years ago derided *faculty* for: namely, as having no desire to seek or develop what faculty profess as adequate, admirable and "imitable" young persons! Most astonishingly, students today still find faculty, for the most part, emotionally inept, intellectually sterile, and especially irrelevant to their lives. But in the topsy-turvy world of the academic establishment and the poster industry over the last two decades, it is an irrelevancy turned completely inside out. Clecak sensed an irrelevancy of "being" in the student critiques of faculty during the heady days of campus unrest and political agitation. Students today, pounding the career fast-track, are much more likely to dismiss faculty, instead, with an irrelevancy of "doing," a perception that professors, in the humanities and social sciences in particular, are cut off from "the regular world," alien to the status quo, too politically and ideologically supercharged, incomprehensibly theoretical, out of the real action, and, hence, totally irrelevant as "imitable adults." That conflict of relevancies is painfully present in the Kent State sociology class on Utopian Societies when students argue in favor of the incentives and rewards accruing to a professional class of doctors and lawyers, while the professor struggles awkwardly to explain the intrinsic satisfactions of doctoring and "being a Ph.D." before degenerating into confused, cynical self-contradiction.

FALAFEL STANDS TO TANNING SALONS

The glacial changes in the tenor of academic life that my generation has both witnessed and inspired can be seen most vividly by contrasting the parasitic institutions that have always clustered around campus fringes like commercial barnacles. Twenty years ago campus environs were encrusted with falafel stands, co-ops, bookstores, coffeehouses, and head shops. Today: Taco Bells, T-shirt emporiums, copy house franchises, chicken-wings joints, and the ubiquitous tanning salon. Such trivialities underscore larger and more meaningful changes in institutional life that reflect cultural shifts away from a communal orientation to a new consumption-oriented corporate establishment. Even in its own small way, the evolution from falafel stands to tan-in-the-cans illustrates a paradigmatic shift that Jürgen Habermas, in the influential *Lifeworld and System* (1981), tracks away from crumbling "Lifeworld" structures (family, parish, synagogue, civic associations) to ascendant "Systemworld" bureaucracies, vehicles to status, wealth, professional expertise, and career mobility that reward today's professors as much as they inspire today's students in their fast-track baccalaureate worlds of food systems delivery and turfgrass management.

In 1964, Mario Savio, the leader of the Free Speech Movement at the University of California, Berkeley, waxed incessantly in sit-in speeches about a "community of love" engendered among students tired of the alienation between faculty and the student body brought on by a post-Sputnik retooling of higher education into the new superefficient megaversity—sprawling, specialized, microengineered, depersonalized—that I entered in fall 1966, an integer in a vast sea of other freshman units. Fast-forward to 1991 and the zebra-coded corporate model that now dominates campus life, a model in which very few students are in the least troubled, much less question, the student/faculty separation that prevails everywhere on campuses fractured and shrink-wrapped into what philosopher of science Stephen Toulmin calls "specialized modes of abstraction": divisions, units, programs, task forces, departments, and committees where, he writes in *The Return to Cosmology*

(1982), "broad and general questions about . . . 'interrelatedness' . . . have been superseded by other, more specialized, disciplinary questions."

That evolution from community to corporation, from interrelatedness and generalization to subspecialization and efficiency, can also be seen in prevailing styles of scholarship, especially in the humanities, and the connection—or, as the case may be now, the radical *disconnection*—between what faculty authors write and what students read. During the falafel era, a high-water table of scholarship, much of it produced by certified academics, fed the springs of undergraduate bookshelves. Upon reflection, the bibliography looks remarkably eclectic, if not terribly resilient, and includes familiar names like Marshall McLuhan, Noam Chomsky, Herbert Marcuse, Theodore Roszak, Susan Sontag, Alvin Toffler, and Rachel Carson, along with less well known authors like George Leonard and William Irvin Thompson and even some transgenerational intellectuals like C. Wright Mills, Dwight MacDonald, Louis Mumford, Michael Harrington, and Jane Jacobs, many of whom were decidedly anti-academic-establishment but whose work could hardly be considered nonscholarly or intellectually dumbed down. Consider, for example, Norman O. Brown's *Love's Body.* Unsurpassed in erudition, Brown's book made a tremendous impact on college campuses when first published in 1966. It was read and discussed widely by faculty *and* undergraduates. Brown's integration of philosophical discourse, literary analysis, and psychoanalytic investigation, played out against the backdrop of intellectual history and cultural politics, established a model of interdisciplinary scholarship—insightful, coherent, relevant, and above all *readable*—that would fall out of fashion in the late seventies when "interdisciplinary" suddenly became synonymous with "undisciplined" or "unspecialized." Today it is virtually impossible to identify a work of contemporary academic scholarship that is known, much less read, by even a narrow swath of undergraduates. (Allan Bloom's *The Closing of the American Mind* naturally comes to mind, although I have yet to meet an undergraduate who's actually read it, much less quarrels with its conclusions. While not strictly interdisciplinary, recent books by Deborah Tannen and Stephen Hawking are rare exceptions that prove the rule.) Interdisciplinary scholarship on the order of *Love's Body* has given way to a species of metacritical discourse practiced by a fairly tight circle of theoretically inclined, annoyingly self-referential, and unwriterly academic superstars whose work remains cloistered in the netherworld of advanced graduate theory seminars convened at advanced humanities institutes, marooned on lists of works cited or in the reduced fonts where academic immortality resides, cryogenically suspended in databases. In lieu of *Of Grammatology*—among the humanities professoriate a much lionized but mind-numbing theoretical tract by French intellectual Jacques Derrida—today's undergraduates opt for clarity in their reading, like Matt Groenig's phenomenally successful cartoon collections—*School Is Hell,* for example—depicting school life as a values wasteland and adulthood generally as a grinding, laughable bore. Or nicely packaged business primers that fuse entrepreneurial savvy and the cult of personality into potent best sellers, like Thomas Peters and Robert Waterman Jr.'s *In Search of Excellence,* or *The Seven Habits of Highly Effective People* by Steven Covey. Meanwhile, pitched battles flare up around campus over such things as canon revision, curriculum reform, phallocratic culture, logocentric signifiers, and the social construction of human consciousness.

Whether post-Sputnik baby boomers took the push for "relevancy" in education seriously or not, at least they listened intently to radical critiques of their schooling during a decade when discussions about educational reform were acrimonious, heated, usually prickly, sometimes otiose, but they never seemed to run cold. Radical reformers like Paul Goodman (*Compulsory Mis-Education*), Charles Silberman (*Crisis in the Classroom*), and Paulo Freire (*Pedagogy of the Oppressed*) fanned the reform discourse so effectively because they treated the school environment not, like today, as a boot camp for American corporations, but as a place where the demands of the society met the needs of individuals in a creative and critical tension. To Goodman and the others, school needed to become an ontological moratorium for young persons when identity and duty—the *termini ad quem* of moral and social life—could be hammered out through a humane conflict between students and the environing polity. "The current movements of rebellion, especially those of youth," Freire wrote, "manifest in their essence [a] preoccupation with men as beings in the world and with the world—a preoccupation with *what* and *how* they are 'being'" (43). Paul Goodman blasted the educational establishment because the bureaucratic machinery of the modern school had come to resemble less a moral encounter between student and status quo and more an administration of the status quo itself, like a department store where students were customers, the curriculum was the merchandise, and the teachers comprised the sales force. Charles Silberman best summed up the agitation for school reform as a *humanizing* of education when he wrote, "Education should prepare people not just to earn a living but to live a life—a creative, humane, and sensitive life" (114). It hardly seems fair or even useful to contrast Goodman's, Silberman's, and Freire's critiques of schooling with Matt Groenig's and his pointy-headed cartoon clones who thumb their noses at substitute teachers and celebrate themselves as underachievers.

INDIVIDUATION TO APPRENTICESHIP

In the nineties, the ethic that powers the raison d'être of schooling in our society has been, once again, completely inverted from Silberman's humanizing model and its understanding of school as a place to individuate into an apprentice model and its treatment of schooling more as a process of matriculating into a career. Paul Goodman's polis has been elbowed out by The Donald's office penthouse as the symbolic venue for the examined life. Once conceived of as an institution that "leads out," school has increasingly become a place that "leads to." It is this transmutation of driving spirit from "being" to "doing" that is partly responsible, I believe, for the current discontinuity of generational commitments and the gradual desensitizing of moral discourse I find among my own students. The values mismatch in the undergraduate classroom is accompanied by a new fascination with applied management theories and techniques among administrators struggling to redefine the academic mission in an era of shrinking resources, a time of capital campaigns, strategic thinking, retooling, downsizing, and total quality management. Meanwhile, the distinction between academic and vocational education begins to blur as professional educationists cozy up to industry captains. University business parks are as commonplace as the revolving door between the university presidency and the corporate board-room. Academic superstars are traded like NBA players. The much-rued extinction of the "public intellectual" in America has given way to a dubious new class of academic celebrities like Stanley Fish and Camille Paglia steered through the campus lecture circuit by publicity agents at a few grand a pop. There is no serious competition for the resume and the memorandum as the most popular genre among undergraduates.

In short, Cardinal Newman's claim in his mid-nineteenth-century classic on liberal education, *The Idea of a University*, that knowledge is its own end no longer anchors the social contract of liberal learning in today's university. Instead, "applied learning" is the new idiom of educational accountability that fuses classroom and workplace into a trajectory of pedagogical competencies stressing teamwork, problem solving, metacognition, time management, resource allocation, outcomes and exit exams, and, generally, the ubiquitous litmus of vocational relevancy—what one observer has called "workplace correctness."

This moral turn from being to doing, or from reflection to consumption, also helps explain the lowering threshold of boredom and tolerance that students today bring to the liberal arts generally. Traditionally the animating spirit of education, the liberal arts disciplines have become instead the animus of undergraduate life. Students today, for the most part, revile a liberal arts curriculum. It has become a barrier to the real work of an undergraduate education: securing gainful—and one hopes meaningful—work in "the regular world." The denigration of liberal arts among today's students wouldn't be nearly so disturbing if the liberal arts consisted only of a knowledge base that spanned the humanistic disciplines, growing (admittedly) more irrelevant by the day. But a liberal arts education concerns more the *context* of a learning experience than the *content* of a curriculum, more an epistemology, indeed an axiology, than a discrete course of study either multicultural or Anglocentric. A liberal education trains and shapes an individual's attitude toward learning itself. A liberal education prepares one to grapple with the crises of distraction and disinterest that become the real adversaries of adult life and citizenship in a consumer society and an information age. The liberal arts disciplines teach self-education and establish patterns of lifelong learning. Consequently, they cultivate the capacity, desire, and drive for independent learning. A liberal education teaches us how to dig out what we need to know, and how to assess what's worth knowing, from the blizzard of irrelevant trivia and disinformation that constantly surrounds us. A liberal education teaches us to think for ourselves, independent of the opinions of others, yet at the same time squaring our own needs and aims in the world with the aspirations of others. "The lesson educators can teach," writes Amy Gutmann in *Democratic Education* (1987), an assessment of the liberal arts tradition and its contributions to "moral education," "is how to publicly defend one's convictions and simultaneously respect the convictions of others with whom one reasonably disagrees" (90). Moreover, these pragmatic and moral considerations are underpinned by the ethical claim of liberalism itself. "The vision behind liberalism," Charles Frankel (*The Case for Modern Man,* 1956) said on the threshold of the nuclear age, "is the vision of a world progressively redeemed by human power from its classic ailments of poverty, disease, and ignorance" (Lasch 1991, 43). As David Bromwich recently notes in a powerful meditation on learning, morality, and tradition, the solidarity of generations is also a formative virtue of a liberal education. Liberalism enfolds personal autonomy and commitment to others into a social ethic that joins, Bromwich writes in *Politics by Other Means* (1992), "what is good for me with what is good for others in the long run" (152).

"Unfortunate is the youth," Jacques Maritain lamented in *Art and Scholasticism,* "who does not know the pleasure of the spirit and is not exalted in the joy of knowing and the joy of beauty, the enthusiasm for ideas, and quickening experience in the first love, delight and luxury of wisdom and poetry" (Smith 1990, 152). The liberal arts, then, is about pleasure, exaltation, joy, enthusiasm, delight, social justice, responsibility, conviction, and commitment, along with the luxury—what St. Augustine called a "learned unhurriedness"—of knowing those things in life that are, from a strictly utilitarian standpoint, *completely useless.* And *realizing that those things are worth knowing.*

Maritain's claim for the intrinsic satisfactions of liberal learning, Frankel's liberal progressivism, and Bromwich's and Gutmann's communitarian ethic might be dismissed by most students today as either incredibly hokey or hopelessly idealistic. That deft dismissal is cued by combined forces, both within the university itself and outside in the society at-large, that have virtually transmogrified the spirit of higher education during the past twenty years and inverted the liberal ideal of the university as an institution of reflection, exploration, and observation, into the corporate view of the university as a place of action, application, praxis, profit, and personal aggrandizement. That inversion of attitude toward learning and its consequent impact on liberal education in America was vividly illustrated by a column in my own campus newspaper that, not coincidentally, appeared during the early blush of the antishanty movement in People's Park. Written by the paper's sports editor, the column applauded the decline of liberal arts disciplines. The writer vigorously defended the triumph of "the hard sciences" as "a change for the better" among undergraduates competing for "jobs, wages and luxurious lifestyles." Sports writers are known for their effective metaphors. His column is punched up with some fine metaphors, like the shiny new engineering building contrasted with the musty old basement with a crumbly ceiling where the philosophy department is housed. Such geomoral constructions reveal, to his mind, truly meaningful status valuations. "Do the rantings and ravings of a few dead poets and philosophers," he asks rhetorically, "mean anything in today's world? The 21st century is coming fast and those who are successful will be on the cutting edge. The connoisseurs of modern art don't care about discipline. They don't learn anything. They don't teach anything. They don't *do* anything." A relentless pounding is capped off by the sports writer's coup de grâce: arts and letters majors don't *earn* much, "unless," he rabbit-punches, "they spend more time at grad school getting a Ph.D., which," he has it on good authority and by living example, "my history professor warned me is 'the quickest and surest way to destroy your brain.'"

REFERENCES

Bloom, Allan. 1987. *The Closing of the American Mind: How Higher Education Has Failed Democracy and Impoverished the Souls of Today's Students*. New York: Simon and Schuster.

Bromwich, David. 1992. *Politics by Other Means: Higher Education and Group Thinking*. New Haven: Yale University Press.

Brown, Norman O. 1966. *Love's Body*. New York: Random House.

Clecak, Peter. 1983. *America's Quest for the Ideal Self: Dissent and Fulfillment in the 60s and 70s*. New York: Oxford University Press.

Frankel, Charles. 1956. *The Case for Modern Man*. New York: Harper.

Freire, Paolo. 1970. *Pedagogy of the Oppressed*. Trans. Myra Bergman Ramos. New York: Herder and Herder.

Gutmann, Amy. 1987. *Democratic Education*. Princeton: Princeton University Press.

Habermas, Jürgen. 1987. *Lifeworld and System: A Critique of Functionalist Reason*. Trans. Thomas McCarthy. Boston: Beacon Press.

Lasch, Christopher. 1991. *The True and Only Heaven: Progress and Its Critics*. New York: W.W. Norton.

Maritain, Jacques. 1930. *Art and Scholasticism: With Other Essays*. Trans. J. F. Scanlan. New York: C. Scribner's Sons.

National Commission on Excellence in Education. 1983. *A Nation at Risk: Report to the Nation and the Secretary of Education, United States Department of Education*. Washington, DC: The Commission.

Postman, Neil. 1985. *Amusing Ourselves to Death: Public Discourse in the Age of Show Business*. New York: Viking.

Smith, Page. 1990. *Killing the Spirit: Higher Education in America*. New York: Viking.

Silberman, Charles. 1970. *Crisis in the Classroom: The Remaking of American Education*. New York: Random House.

Toulmin, Stephen. 1982. *The Return to Cosmology: Postmodern Science and the Theology of Nature*. Berkeley: University of California Press.

ACADEMIC PROFESSIONALISM
AND THE BETRAYAL OF THE
LAND-GRANT TRADITION (1999)

BEFORE PASSAGE OF FEDERAL LEGISLATION INAUGURATING THE LAND-grant movement in the 1860s, elite private colleges enjoyed an educational monopoly that exclusively served America's professional classes. These were colleges that Justin Morrill, father of the land-grant acts, subtly denigrated as "literary institutions" (Parker 1924, 262), by which he implied effete seats of privilege. The land-grant college was supposed to offer an alternative that embodied a passionate feeling for democracy, access, and educational pragmatism: the open road of American higher learning, egalitarian, energetic, and free.

I wish to argue, however, that this conceptual framework situating egalitarianism and class privilege as the organizing polarities of American higher education history is misleading. Instead, *professionalism*—along with an entire cultural complex evoked by the mystique of professionalization—long ago displaced a vigorous if oversimplified democratic ideology as the driving force behind American land-grant colleges. "The Professional Complex," as Talcott Parsons pointed out in the 1950s, had long dominated the university ethos and rendered obsolete late-nineteenth-century standards of institutional self-definition such as liberty and equality or, indeed, the class perquisites of social privilege, style, and taste. Arguing that professionalism had become the crucial structural component of modern society, Parsons concluded that "the academic emphasis is now much more on achievement criteria and on reputation in a national and international cultural forum" (1967, 542) than on the philosophical dialectic suggested by the land-grant and the elite Ivy League models. Further inquiry shows, in fact, that the new academic professionalism, according to one line of argument, is quite old. Barely a generation separates Morrill's Land-Grant Act, passed into law in 1862, from Thorstein Veblen's early twentieth-century attacks on university administrators he called "captains of erudition" (1946, 62) whom he blamed for turning universities into professional/commercial bureaucracies fundamentally no different than banks and breakfast cereal manufacturers obsessed with profit, status, and prestige. Veblen's critique cut across any meaningful distinctions that could be made between a Harvard or Princeton and premier land-grant universities like Cornell and UC Berkeley. According to Burton Bledstein, "For the past three quarters of a century, the debate about the nature of American higher education has continued to be conducted in Veblen's terms" (1976, 288).

Instead of standing opposed across an ideological Maginot Line separating democratic egalitarianism from the privileges accruing to social class, land-grant colleges and elite universities march, then, to the *same* drummer, to the same beat, as Bledstein puts it, of "the ego-satisfying pretensions of professionalism" (1976, 289).

THE SUBVERSION OF LAND-GRANT IMPERATIVES

The original imperative undergirding the land-grant movement rested in a moral conception consistent with Thomas Jefferson's yeoman republicanism, an ideology that fused education, liberty, and civil society into a politico-ethical holism (Nevins 1962, 16–17). The land-grant movement represents a characteristic, if not classic, American melding of can-do pragmatism and lofty democratic idealism into a vision of education as *the* great social equalizer. Innervated by the defining virtues of democratic humanism and driven by an unbending faith in progress and America's reckless appetite for frontier expansion, the central ideas driving the land-grant movement included liberty and equality, freedom of opportunity, the leveling of geographic and class barriers to higher education, unrestricted access to all occupations, and the application of knowledge and technology to the civic sphere.

It is not so much the failure of the land-grant college to live up to such values that has emboldened, even outraged, critics. The acerbic criticism of a moralist like Wendell Berry is directed more at the ease with which land-grant schools have methodically subverted a strapping egalitarianism as their defining character by uncritically adopting a new-style professionalism synonymous with utilitarianism in the service of power, status, and prestige: in short, a wholesale shift in institutional values. The history of the land-grant college, according to Berry, has been a story of the surrender of institutional standards and self-definition in which liberal and practical education gives way to specialized curricula that serve narrower and narrower professional constituencies. If this evolution, Berry considers, "has not been caused by, it has certainly accompanied a degeneration of faculty standards, by which professors and teachers of disciplines become first upholders of 'professional standards' and then careerists in pursuit of power, money, and prestige" (1977, 147).

The original intent of land-grant legislation also stressed the creation of regional institutions that would be shaped by and responsive to local conditions, local problems, and local needs. "What we have instead," Berry observes, "is a system of institutions which more and more resemble one another, like airports and motels, made increasingly uniform by the transience or rootlessness of their career-oriented faculties and the consequent inability to respond to local conditions. The professor lives in his career, in a ghetto of career-oriented fellow professors" (147).

PROFESSIONALISM AS AN ETHICAL CONDITION

It is frequently argued that *professional* education—curricula, that is to say, in the service of occupational specializations such as the "mechanics arts," agriculture, law, and medicine—has always been the main thrust of the land-grant college, certainly not its nemesis. The debate over the failure or the fruition of the land-grant movement is, for the most part, then, an important debate over definitions of professionalism and especially the ideological valences carried by particular usages of the term. Wendell Berry, for one, does not use "professionalization" within a strictly denotative and tightly circumscribed context where it is interchangeable with "occupational specialization." Critics like Berry rarely quarrel with any reference to "professional" as a vocational category delineating basic elements of performance and behavior: for example, technical or managerial expertise, disinterestedness, meticulousness, command of and commitment to task, coolness under fire, and so on. These are processes and traits associated with the *activities* of the professional.

The systematic betrayal of the land-grant mission rued by social critics from Thorstein Veblen to Richard Ohmann and Berry is rooted in a much different connotation. In this latter usage, "professionalism" is understood to be an ethical condition, an ethos, and a process of socialization and cultural differentiation that leads to, and legitimizes, institutional meritocracy, monopoly, exclusion, privilege, and the special perquisites accorded to title, status, and rank: that is, authoritarian social forms totally anathema to the land-grant ethic of egalitarianism. Burton Bledstein traces the critique of professionalism as a socioethical condition to a lineage of critics who see "in the professions a spectacle of knowledge, a presentation of false universals in a bourgeois ideology that terminated rationality in the 'incorporation' of authoritarian social forms. . . . By means of the skills of public impression management, professionals promoted the unreality of personal ideals such as autonomy, self-control, and mastery while serving to conceal the reality of private, corporate power." For these critics, Bledstein continues, "professional roles made possible the deviancy of socialization at the highest levels of power and wealth. Those roles legitimized privilege, legally sanctioned opportunity in the upper middle class, certified an elite selected by qualities other than merit, and legally put in place institutions served by professionals that made ordinary citizens pay for a social system that did not work for them" (1985, 5).

Bledstein argues that class-based authoritarian professionalism has both supplied the values and provided the managerial arrangements to American universities since at least 1870. In fact, the university has served as an incubator, Bledstein maintains, for the kind of cultural values and practices eagerly sought after by an energetic and upwardly mobile middle class. Such values and practices include "careerism, competition, the standardization of rules and the organization of hierarchies, the obsession with expansion and growth, professionals seeking recognition and financial rewards for their efforts, [and] administrators in the process of building empires" (1976, 288–289)—to which one might add, given the contemporary university's leading position in the global marketplace, the production and manipulation of information and the willingness on the part of its academic professionals to follow the call of opportunity no matter where it may lead. Far from being a place where moral gravity runs against utilitarian currents of human self-enclosure and self-interest, the American university, notwithstanding the ethical pretensions of its land-grant heritage, has long been a haven for Captains of Erudition. "In the professional atmosphere of the American University," Bledstein concedes, "eager Americans related within themselves to their private desire for distinction, and to independence from the commonplace and the average. They related beyond themselves to the next highest rung on the vocational ladder, to the canons of the profession set forth by the elders, to the last link of the great chain stringing together a career, and to the honorary and material rewards that accompanied success" (1976, 309).

THE PROFESSIONAL COMPLEX AS A POSTMODERN HABITAT

The incompatibility—indeed, the *contradiction*—between the land-grant heritage and Bledstein's culture of professionalism reveals three fundamental issues essential, I believe, to any meaningful debate about contemporary higher education in America.

First, professional and vocational practices—what Bruce Wilshire calls "academic rites of purification and exclusion" (1990, 97)—support an academic meritocracy that undermines the populist mystique inherent in the land-grant mission. A democratic ethos inferred by the admittedly imprecise but unequivocally high-principled language of the Morrill Act itself, in which land-grant colleges were enjoined "to promote the liberal and practical education of the industrial classes" (Morrill 1964, 145), is everywhere compromised by "the ego-satisfying pretensions of professionalism" to which faculties have so effortlessly succumbed.

Second, the much-discussed, hands-wringing debate over curriculum reform, multiculturalism, and canon-revision conducted along the various fronts of the academic culture wars and served up in today's popular and intellectual press as ideologically inspired and politically driven is a debate, on the contrary, that completely camouflages the deep-rooted elitism that remains the cultural condition of the modern university.

Finally, the Professional Complex has become a natural habitat for postmodern theories of culture and critical practice that currently prevail in the academic humanities, which I will turn to in more detail below. Briefly, those theories are anchored in common epistemological, ontological, and sociological nostrums. Knowledge and truth, for example, are always contingent and forever relative, thereby opening up the field of interpretation to virtually limitless critical franchises. Next, identity is a social construction subject to the manipulation of prevailing and privileged classes and groups. Social authority, meanwhile, is inherently predatory and rapacious. As modes of critical disciplinary self-reflection, the mushrooming proliferation of theories constituting "postmodernism" proper owe their legitimacy—especially, if not solely, in the humanities—to professional interests of the academic meritocracy while neglecting the social application

74

and civic impact of academic work, a point hammered home in Richard Rorty's devastating excoriation of postmodern intellectuals in a 1991 *Dissent* essay and the subject of his latest book, *Achieving Our Country* (1998). The wholesale neglect of "application"—an ethical bulwark of land-grant pedagogy—prompts a noted literary critic to complain about the "arid and unreal" material cranked out by a theory industry completely "out of touch with human needs and interests." "There are so many theorists," according to William Cain, "all of whom are devotedly pursuing the latest fads and processing the most current methodologies, that questions of value and significance are rarely asked. To ask such questions would, one feels, disrupt the marketplace, where reputations are established and inertly accepted, and where there is little time for reflection upon the point and purpose of theoretical labor" (1984, xi).

In assessing the cumulative effects of postmodern thinking on professional standards, especially within the land-grant college, I am primarily concerned with the moral realm where private aspirations engage the larger professional community, and where personal career identity and responsibilities to public life are worked out among a community of fellow practitioners. When I speak of academic professionalism as a moral issue, I am thinking, in particular, of how to reconcile the quest for self-purpose, aspiration, commitment, and self-respect—the larger rhythms, in other words, of an individual moral life—against those *institutional* standards by which the profession regards us and, by extension, trains us to regard ourselves. That reconciliation is complicated by an uneasy partnership in academe, at no time more strained than now, between teaching and scholarship: between teaching, that is to say, as a fundamentally altruistic activity—a giving of oneself, freely, to another—and the self-aggrandizement especially characteristic of postmodern scholarship and scholarly practices in an era when private life is dominated, indeed overwhelmed, by what Jürgen Habermas (1981) calls Systemsworld institutions, monolithic professional organizations—such as, in my fields, the Modern Language Association and the American Studies Association—that merge boundaries of personal and professional identity and tend to blur role distinctions between the public intellectual and the self-reflexive academic celebrity.

"Evolution," writes Erik Erikson in his seminal study of identity formation, "has made [human beings] teaching as well as . . . learning animal[s], for dependency and maturity are reciprocal: mature [men and women] need . . . to be needed, and maturity," Erikson wisely notes, "is guided by the nature of that which must be cared for" (1968, 138). For those persons who may have entered into an academic career searching for an avenue of Erikson's reciprocity between dependency and self-fulfillment, the current professional climate, culminating from the trends of the past twenty years, renders that mutuality difficult, if not impossible, to attain. Since teaching itself, as Bruce Wilshire argues, can no longer be "a fundamental value in the university as it is presently constituted" (1990, 79), the generativity that Erikson regards as essential to individuation is refused and everywhere frustrated by the competitiveness and status anxiety that presently tax academic life and make any discussion of the land-grant tradition's promise or current performance seem irrelevant. The great gift of guiding others that leads to *self*-completion—what Erikson calls "an expansion of ego-interests"—has been superseded by the tenuous rewards of professional accomplishment in which one is praised and promoted for publishing highly specialized research and implicitly denigrated, indeed often punished, for fulfilling the university's end of the social contract. Teaching—not to mention the even less worn path of public service—simply put, has become a fatality on the road to academic success. The "expansion of ego-interests" achieved through teaching's altruistic creativity has given way, regrettably, to a *contraction* of ego-interests that accompanies the clamber for display, recognition, self-promotion, and fame in the contemporary university that Emerson, in "The American Scholar," warned was inimical to the moral enterprise of a university education.

I do not mean to sound the alarmist claim that if you were to bore into the center of academic culture today you would find nothing but moral rot. I do believe, however, that higher education is in crisis, and that the professoriate's growing alienation from the undergraduate classroom, along with the easy surrender of ethical traditions like land-grant egalitarianism in favor of the tenuous rewards of careerism among today's fast-track academics, have contributed to that crisis. Those failings must be redressed in order to recover what a university can be from what it has become.

The university's alienation from the open road of public life has been rued by a surging chorus of critics from both inside and outside academe as different as Lynne Cheney, Page Smith, Camille Paglia, and Ernest Boyer. Among the professoriate, meanwhile, higher and higher levels of critical bravado, credential posturing, institutional migration, and professional development tactics further widen the gaping chasm between theory and practice that the land-grant college historically set out to bridge. Institutional loyalty, commitment to practices that engage one as a participant in the collective life of a college or university, the pursuit of a scholarship of application that impacts the larger society as well as local communities, and the interplay of professional duty and communal memory are as rare in academe as they have always been in the National Basketball Association, the organization most frequently cited when analyzing today's academic meritocracy. Instead, the worship of merit and position—independent of institutional *commitment* but more and more tied to institutional *affiliation*—presently obtains in the anxious world of academic sweepstakes. The poet John Hollander's indictment of the academic professional bears quoting: "The *gauchisme* of many younger scholars reads like the deeply unpolitical cant of an exceedingly careerist generation. Many of the scholars wielding disproportionate power . . . in the universities today have the same character as CEOs who look only for the quarterly bottom line, as lawyers who have been contriving to give that profession an even—did it seem possible—worse name" (1991, 11).

SPANNING THE CHASM BETWEEN THE
ACADEMIC AND PUBLIC LIFE

Given the prevailing corporate paradigm, is it possible to reinvigorate the desiccated roots of land-grant liberalism? Can a quiescent civic populism, the historic lifeblood of the land-grant heritage, check the virus of academic professionalism that courses through today's culture of higher learning?

In spite of their intemperate overstatement, such questions, and the arguments they raise, are not irrelevant, especially to midcareer academic baby boomers typically ambivalent about turning to the past but increasingly anxious over where we seem to be headed, reluctant to slip into the free fall of disbelief offered by their thirtysomething postmodernist colleagues—a generation crowding fifty that finds itself, to borrow from Mathew Arnold's "Stanzas from the Grand Chartreuse," "Wandering between two worlds, one dead, / The other powerless to be born."

The questions posed above may seem less daunting, however, when one considers that the recent institutional history of academic professionalism is, notwithstanding Veblen's scorching critique of the Captains of Erudition in 1918, at odds with the civic culture that gave rise to modern structures of higher learning. Civic duty and academic professionalization, after all, worked in partnership during nineteenth-century innovations in higher education. Graduate schools, in particular at Hopkins, Columbia, and elsewhere, sought to train advanced students in an intellectual regimen designed to prepare them for careers in civil service and the duties of public life generally. That partnership continued during the high-water period of the Progressive Era when a new generation of intellectuals were especially wary of becoming marooned in a genteel academic culture. The importance of knowledge tuned to social engagement informed, for example, the philosophic pragmatism of William James and John Dewey. The vision of an academic intellect pressed to social inquiry gave rise to a service ideal that inspired great universities during the first two decades of the present century, notably the University of Chicago and the University of Wisconsin. Public culture, in a word, was a natural habitat of the intellect. Academic professionalism and civic life formed an ecology that nourished a generation of academic/public intellectuals anxious for contact and communication with the educated public.

Further, in questioning how to reinvigorate the land-grant tradition, it is important to keep foremost in mind that the discontinuity between academic expertise and civic culture is a recent aberration arising partly, I believe, out of the Möbius loop of postmodernist sensibility that informs contemporary academic professionalism, especially in the arts and humanities disciplines. Academic postmodernism, as I mentioned above, rests on fundamental epistemological, sociological, and linguistic claims, including an explicit prohibition against universal truths, a skepticism over any call to connectivity and consensus in the arena of social action, and an outright rejection of an Enlightenment discourse that privileges such humanist tropes as "the social contract," "the public good," and "the common welfare." The strong ideological position staked out in some new humanities subfields, for example, is heavily colored by postmodern skepticism over the possibilities for integrating theory and social action. In particular, the democratic ties that bind individual lives to the common welfare are now viewed, through the skeptical lens of postmodernism, as political shackles that oppress. A shared body of moral values that integrates a curriculum into a social order threatens to become, we are warned, a pretense for domination by privileged classes and groups. Moreover, a curriculum that aims for balance, commonality, and synthesis, according to postmodern pedagogy, is really no different than a curriculum that seeks to eradicate differences, thereby reinforcing ethnocentrism, cultural hegemony, and class oppression.

Postmodernism offers a new sensibility, then, that reifies *separation* in its understanding of the relation between self and other. In its appeal to skepticism, its moral and ontological vacuity, its chronic subjectivity, and its disdain for middle-class culture, postmodernism eschews any appeal to transcendent sources of value, preferring instead an immanence that sometimes borders on obsessive self-enclosure. The humanist ideal of a shared civic culture and the accompanying ethical claims of individuals obligated and actively committed to the common welfare—the yoking together, in other words, of political liberalism and moral pragmatism into a democratic humanism that remains the base element of the land-grant ethic—become, to the postmodernist mind, mere ideological claims "socially constructed," at best, and, at worst, epistemological weapons in the service of those who seek to maintain cultural hegemony.

In its refusal to seek or acknowledge a common ground for life's deepest moral and political decisions, academic postmodernism denies the humanist, in particular, the liberal intellectualism and the civic empathy necessary to maintain the ethical vitality of a land-grant institution that grows out of its commitment to the application of knowledge in the civic sphere. It follows that a revitalization of the land-grant tradition requires nothing less than a rebuilding of the social personae of the academic professions not on the logic of commercial free agency or through the spiritually empty traces of theory, but in the language of ethics. The rudiments of that project, as noted in a 1987 Hastings Center report on professional ethics and the public role of the academic professional, "may be found [already] in the ethical traditions of many of the professions today." In calling for a strengthening of those ethical traditions, the report concludes "to be a professional is to be dedicated to a distinctive set of ideals and standards of conduct. It is to lead a certain kind of life defined by special virtues and norms of character. And it is to enter into a subcommunity with a characteristic moral ethos and outlook" (Jennings, Callahan, and Wolf 1987, 5).

I am heartened to see a resurgence of interest in civic humanism and social capital in the serious intellectual work of long-established scholars throughout the humanities and social sciences, especially during a time guided by the communitarian public policies of President Clinton. I am particularly pleased to witness a renewed interest in public culture, broadly defined, among those of my own generation. Rich in "moral ethos and outlook," such work, entirely compatible with the land-grant agenda, is compelled by the postmodernist alternative of radical disconnection of academic practitioners from their public roles and responsibilities and the ethical content of their scholarly discourses. Situated within the ethical canons of professional disciplinary practices, those discourses form the "linchpins of public trust in a profession," to cite again the Hastings Center report. "They give professionalism its moral dimension; they transform the career of selling services into the calling of providing services" (Jennings 1987, 3). Scholarship that resonates with and advances the moral ethos of its particular professional and disciplinary culture is not only essential to an honest assessment of the contemporary land-grant university and its failure or fruition. Without such work, any dialogue over the renewal of the land-grant ethic is itself pointless.

Any discussion of the revitalization or retooling of the land-grant college, I mean to suggest, cannot take place in the absence of a postmodernist critique. Nor can that discussion avoid entering a moral venue that concerns the relation of an individual academic expert to her or his common civic culture where institutions are historically situated. My own criticisms of academic professionalization, then, have less to do with the legitimacy of academic expertise or specialization. My criticisms concern the strained relationship between the academic expert and public life mediated by institutions and their collective values, commitments, and the sense of shared destiny felt, and felt deeply, among their worker/citizens.

REFERENCES

Berry, Wendell. 1977. *The Unsettling of America: Culture and Agriculture.* San Francisco: Sierra Club Books.

Bledstein, Burton. 1976. *The Culture of Professionalism: The Middle Class and the Development of Higher Education in America.* New York: Norton.

———. 1985. "Professions, Professionals, Professionalism." *Prospects: An Annual of American Culture Studies* 10: 1–15.

Cain, William. 1984. *The Crisis in Criticism: Theory, Literature, and Reform in English Studies.* Baltimore: Johns Hopkins University Press.

Erikson, Erik. 1968. *Identity: Youth and Crisis.* New York: Norton.

Habermas, Jürgen. 1981. *Lifeworld and System: A Critique of Functionalist Reason.* Trans. Thomas McCarthy. Boston: Beacon Press.

Hollander, John. 1991. "Reading As Never Was Read." *ADE Bulletin* 98: 7–13.

Jennings, B., D. Callahan, and S. Wolf, S. 1987. "The Professions: Public Interest and Common Good." *The Public Duties of the Professions.* Washington, DC: Hastings Center: 3–10.

Morrill Act, Title 7, Section 301. 1964. *United States Code Annotated.* Brooklyn.

Nevins, Alan. 1962. *The State Universities and Democracy.* Urbana: University of Illinois Press.

Parker, William. 1924. *The Life and Public Services of Justin Smith Morrill.* New York: Houghton Mifflin.

Parsons, Talcott. 1967. "Professions." *Encyclopedia of Social Science.* New York: Macmillan.

Rorty, Richard. 1991. "Intellectuals in Politics. Too Far In? Too Far Out?" *Dissent:* 483–490.

―――. 1998. *Achieving Our Country: Leftist Thought in Twentieth-Century America.* Cambridge: Harvard University Press.

Veblen, Thorstein. 1946. *Higher Learning in America.* New York: Viking.

Wilshire, Bruce. 1990. *The Moral Collapse of the University: Professionalism, Purity, and Alienation.* Albany: State University of New York Press.

BUS RIDES AND FORKS IN THE ROAD: THE MAKING OF A PUBLIC SCHOLAR (2002)

One consolation of finishing graduate work during the job market freeze-out in the late 1970s was the opportunity I had to experience, during a single semester, what obliquely struck me at the time as the full institutional spectrum of American postsecondary education. Facing unemployment lines jammed with fellow baby boomer academics and without the slightest prospect for a full-time tenure track position, I managed nonetheless to cobble together three part-time teaching jobs. After covering a couple sections of freshman English at Rhode Island College, I walked a few blocks through a working-class neighborhood in North Providence and caught the in-bound Smith Street bus. I hopped off a few stops later at Providence College, where I taught another Composition course. Back on the bus, I transferred downtown to an East Side bus that groaned up the Benefit Street tunnel past the magisterial Unitarian Church and by blue-blood mansions. The bus dropped me off in front of Brown University's Rockefeller Library, where I presided over a senior seminar in Religious Studies. I dimly imagined the bus ride as a symbolic journey along an institutional axis that defined the organizing polarities of higher learning in America. Even more important, could the bus ride, I wondered, hold the secret to a personal myth that would make some sense out of the fear, second-guessing, and inner turbulence I was feeling at the precarious threshold of a career?

In an odd way that I could not fully understand at the time, the bus ride forced me to navigate an existential tack between the extremes and contradictions of American higher education. There were, after all, none of the obvious restrictions, benefits, or pretensions of social rank at the open-admission state college where I taught Composition that were evident at the highly selective, richly endowed private university among my superbright students in the Religious Studies seminar. At the same time, my working-class students at RIC, even though they fumbled with the rudiments of language and argument in their essays on *Starsky and Hutch*, were struggling (indeed, as I was) with the same perplexities of meaning, identity, and purpose as the Brown students who teased out their insights from the novels of Camus and Georges Bernanos. Meanwhile, to complicate matters, my students at Providence College struck me as secure in a way that neither the RIC students nor their Brown peers showed. Anchored in their Catholic tradition, the PC students' self-questioning, while just as energetic, seemed less open-ended and less edged by ambivalence during discussions about moral and ethical dilemmas that inevitably surfaced in all three classrooms that semester, whether we were probing the finer points in Sartre's *Nausea* or a scene from *Hawaii Five-0*. Thanks to the PC students, I surprised myself with a willingness to defend the role played by institutional heritage, especially in the Brown seminar, where theology and adherence to religious doctrine were often treated like problems instead of solutions.

In any event, I found the challenges and opportunities of that year morally bracing, pedagogically challenging, and intellectually stimulating. I appreciated the populism, the passion for democratic openness, and the educational pragmatism that suffused the climate of Rhode Island College. I respected the commitment to character education at Providence College. I admired the high intellectual standards and extraordinary motivation and drive of my Brown students. Even though I was denied the security, responsibilities, and perquisites of life on the tenure track, the bus ride from North Providence to the East Side was a practical education in what the humanities were all about: commitment to the social witness of ideas, intellectual community, and the arc of hope that scribes the moral lives of students. I felt, naively no doubt, a little like Walt Whitman setting out on the open road of American higher learning . . . egalitarian, energetic, and free.

Nearly a quarter century of experience teaching in a number of liberal arts colleges and public research universities from Rhode Island to California and a few moments of serious midcareer reflection reveal, however, that my symbolic journey may have been, after all, only a bus ride. When I look back, trying to make some sense of the roads I have traveled since the patchwork of temporary teaching jobs in Providence, I see myself, like many other academics of my generation, facing hurdles, hitting roadblocks, wandering up cul de sacs, and eventually nudging into the clear. Most higher education faculty face the same pseudo-predicament as the self-questioning traveler in Robert Frost's much-read and often-misunderstood poem "The Road Not Taken." At some point in our careers we face forks in the road. One route, well paved and maintained, points to scholarship and research. Another leads to teaching. Bending to the underbrush, a third path, barely worn, fades off into service and the faint call of public work. In spite of institutional rituals and appointment, promotion, and tenure bylaws to the contrary, these routes remain, for most intents and purposes, separate pathways. Like Frost's traveler, faculty make their choices and stick to their career paths, "knowing how way leads to way" and doubting "if I shall ever come back" to take a different route.

For my part, I was dogged early on by persistent questions raised by a moribund job market, on the one hand, and a nascent feeling for a dynamic and integrative learning life that stuck with me after the bus ride in Providence, on the other. Could I bring my "whole self" to a vocation in higher education? Could I practice a scholarship that nourished an active inner life while forging strong and meaningful links to the public sphere? What would scholarship, teaching, and service look like if they supported both personal wholeness and the fulfillments of an engaged public life?

The decade of the 1980s was not kind to young academics in the humanities who charted a career course with those questions in mind. At least in
my case, the generative impulses that naturally flow into teaching and service were quickly dammed up by the ethos of professionalism I encountered
after leaving Providence for a string of adjunct teaching appointments from
California and eventually to the upper Midwest. It is a species of professionalism familiar to critics of American higher education throughout the last
century and culminating in our era with critical voices that span a staggering
ideological gamut, from Thomas Sowell to Camille Paglia. Most recently,
culture critic Christopher Lasch, in a collection of bare-knuckle essays
posthumously published in 1994 (*The Revolt of the Elites and the Betrayal
of Democracy*), lamented an educational establishment paralyzed by moral
inertia, theoretical abstraction, and a thinly veiled contempt for the public
outside the academy.

This story of increasing isolation from public life and the prevailing
sanction of professional recognition and reward has been particularly true
of the humanities. A rising chorus of critics from both within and outside
the academy complain about the humanities' abandonment of a historic
mission to democratize public culture and to practice a discourse that illu-
minates and clarifies the moral and ethical dimensions of problems that
beset civic life.

In spite of my youthful idealism and Pollyanna rationalizations, no matter how I sliced it I could not avoid the painful truth that I was setting out
into a profession whose vital signs were bad in 1978. And getting worse.

To compound matters, my liberal education led me to suspect a causal
connection between the decline and discontent that wracked the humanities during the 1980s and 1990s and the loosening of the ligaments of
democracy and civil society witnessed during the same period. "What do
we see," Jean Bethke Elshtain bluntly asks in *Democracy on Trial* (1995), a
sobering analysis of the politics of difference that plagues our democratic
life, "when we look around [today]? We find deepening cynicism; the
growth of corrosive forms of isolation, boredom, and despair; the weakening, in other words, of that world known as democratic civil society, a
world of groups and associations and ties that bind" (4). The power of the

humanistic disciplines, I had been trained to believe during the course of my graduate work in American Studies, lies in their capacities to bridge private lives and public obligations—the inner and outer worlds—and enrich moral life while simultaneously shaping a personal identity responsive to the commitments and responsibilities of citizenship in a democracy. That power has steadily waned during the last two decades only to be replaced by a corrosive academic professionalism that threatens to turn the academy, as Ernest Boyer—quoted by David Brown in a 1995 article, "The Public/ Academic Disconnect," in the Kettering Foundation's *Higher Education Exchange*—puts it, into "a place for faculty to get tenured and students to get credentialed."

So it was against this backdrop that I began to chart a course through academe. It has been, and continues to be, a struggle played out in the moral realm where personal aspirations engage the larger professional community, and where personal career identity and responsibilities to public life are supposed to be worked out among a community of fellow practitioners/seekers. I floundered trying to find ways to reconcile the quest for self-purpose, aspiration, commitment, and self-respect—the larger rhythms, in other words, of an individual moral life—against those standards by which the profession regards me and, by extension, trains me to regard myself.

Like so many academics of my generation, those reconciliations were made difficult by the chronically depressed conditions of an insanely competitive job market in the late 1970s and throughout the 1980s. After leaving Providence for the West Coast, I began my first full-time teaching job on a shoestring contract as a "Visiting Lecturer" in the English department at a large public university. Even though my contract was renewed annually for several years, I remained cut off, it became clear to me from the outset of my appointment, from any hope of ever entering into the tenure system. I would never become a full institutional citizen and peer among the mostly older tenured faculty in the department and the one or two lucky younger ones who had somehow slipped into the tenure stream right out of graduate school. A decade-long houseguest in English (an "academic bracero," as an early program director put it, without wincing), I was beginning to suffer acute ambivalence over what I had gotten myself into. In any event, convinced that I was a would-be scholar and teacher facing a hostile and unforgiving university, my inner world pitched head long into the rapids of early midlife crisis. The institutional alienation and collegial dislocation I felt during that period certainly extracted a serious toll on my professional, personal, and moral life. I was left with a residual cynicism over academic culture that, to this day, wells up on occasion and forces me to practice patience and restraint and seek the counsel of trusted colleagues, old mentors, intimates, and friends. But in spite of the difficult straits I found myself in during my turbulent thirties, nothing succeeded in completely undermining my basic commitment to finding what Thomas Merton called a "quiet but articulate place" where I could dig in, find my voice, and carry on a modest life's work.

In my not remarkable case, that search was, in part, foisted upon me when my visiting lectureship was "disrenewed" in 1988 and I found myself back in the chaotic academic marketplace looking for work. I applied for a million teaching positions. As good fortune would have it, I landed one temporary two-year instructorship at a Midwest university. After fourteen hard years plying the adjunct teaching trade, I was eventually hired into a regular appointment at the same university and awarded tenure within two years. It would be a mistake, however, to conclude that the terms of my professional renewal or emotional survival hinged solely on achieving security of employment. If anything, tenure only raised the stakes. An inner revolution was also taking place, spurred by years of identity confusion, role conflicts, and the inflated self-consciousness that comes from feelings of self-doubt. Granted a new beginning, my identity confusion gradually gave way to renewed purposefulness. I began to feel a pull of intimacy and belonging toward my new university. Integrity slowly replaced despair. An obsession with justice and fair treatment receded against a new awareness of and appreciation for the workings of mercy and good fortune in my life. Promise and possibility appeared on a spiritual horizon once edged by dark feelings of stagnation and entrapment.

During this tumultuous period, I was working on a book about the monk, poet, and social critic Thomas Merton, eventually published in 1989 under the title *Thomas Merton's Art of Denial* (University of Georgia Press). I engaged Merton's extraordinary spiritual and literary journey by tracking his inner conflicts, self-doubts, and ambivalences—a crucible of creative inner tensions that is the wellspring, I argued, of Merton's important message for our own troubled times. In a "Speculative Epilogue" to that book, I tried to retrace Thomas Merton's story using the psychoanalyst Erik Erikson's pioneering work on moral development and identity formation fleshed out in his 1968 book *Identity: Youth and Crisis.* I discovered that the broad outlines of the Merton biography bear marked and interesting similarities to Erikson's stages of identity development. I was especially drawn to the crucial and pivotal period he called the early adulthood identity crisis—a term that has become, unfortunately, much clichéd since Erikson coined it in the 1950s. In his engaging psychological biographies of Martin Luther and Mohandas Gandhi, for example, Erikson focuses on their midlife turmoils. He argues that this period of isolation, withdrawal, and critical inner searching holds the key to understanding the dynamic processes of confused and conflicted young persons successfully negotiating the passage into mature and responsible adulthood. Through his psychoanalytic work, Erikson found that identity conflicts flare up and seek resolution during an identity moratorium of early adulthood. Those conflicts eventually pave the way to living the remaining developmental stages of life unified and reconciled. One is better equipped, Erikson felt, to accept oneself and to embrace with less resignation and ambivalence one's place in society. The midlife identity crisis, in short, shapes and tempers a lasting and durable sense of adult duty. Once resolved, according to Erikson, an individual is ready to engage the balance of the life course with social commitment, caring, personal integrity, and trust.

Standing now on the threshold of my fiftieth birthday, the wisdom and clarity of hindsight reveals an insight that I was not prepared to see during my midthirties when I was writing the Merton book. Simply put, in writing Thomas Merton's story I was entering, albeit in a subliminal way, into my own journey, trying to make sense of my inner conflicts while I was engaging Merton's midlife crisis. By following him into his pitched quarrels with the world around him and the inner fire of his own self-doubts and by engaging his struggle through my writing and research, he served, in effect, as a pilot who helped navigate my parallel inner journey through the shoals and rough waters of midlife crisis. In spite of the difficult straits I found myself in during these unsettled years, nothing succeeded in undermining my basic commitment to writing about Thomas Merton and his struggles to find what he called a "quiet but articulate place" where he too could fit in and carry on his life's work. In return for the emotional and intellectual energy I invested in the Merton book, I found gratification and a sense of inner direction and fulfillment that compensated for—indeed, rescued me from—the unhappiness, futility, and disappointment of my life as an itinerant academic. Looking back, I can appreciate the wisdom of Erik Erikson's claim that during the identity crisis certain individuals dramatize their own crises by projecting them onto creative models of resolution. Among them, Erikson writes in a chapter on "Epigenesis of Identity," are "works of art or . . . original deeds" spun by individuals "eager to tell us all about [their crises] in diaries, letters, and self-representations" or, for me, through biographical narrative. "Even as the neuroses of a given period reflect the ever-present chaos of [a person's] existence . . . , the creative crises point to the period's unique solutions" (134).

In particular, two new coordinates set the trajectory of my changing commitments as a teacher/scholar. First, the role that institutions play in shaping my identity and integrity became more important and obvious. While it is true that institutions sometimes betray us through rejection and, worse, indifference, they can also be, I sensed for the first time, important sources of affirmation, acceptance, and individuation. Second, a unitive spiritual and moral impulse began to inform and shape my intellectual and pedagogical work.

I began to realize that a life—especially a *teaching* life—lived outside of or free from the influence of institutions was more of an impoverishment than a virtue. Institutions of higher learning, by their very nature, shape us in profound ways. I still struggled, sometimes against strong currents stirred by old animosities, to become a better institutional citizen. But I also recognized the reciprocity between my individual strength and the larger mission and health of the public university that now employed me. I took on committee work, tentatively at first. I threw myself into curricular innovation. I shaped courses and learning projects that were consonant with the core values of my new university, a premier land-grant institution. I even answered the call of academic service and took a temporary assignment as a program administrator.

More important, a harmonic drive began to pervade my calling as a teacher, my intellectual interests and worldview, as well as my philosophical inclinations. It was as if a new compass plotted my sense of moral direction. I became compelled to see the world around me and my place in it as a complex network of connections, integrations, balances, couplings, and ties that bind, and not a place of chaos, division, irreconcilable differences, and movement against the grain. Sociobiologist Edward O. Wilson recently jump-started an old philosophical term to describe this condition. Underlying all forms of knowledge and ways of knowing is an urge to unity he calls, in a 1999 book of the same name, "consilience." My new passion for connectivity went far beyond epistemology, however, and spilled over into an ecological lucidity that brought moral fluency across all sorts of boundaries. My teaching, in particular, fell under the influence of what Parker Palmer, in a passionate 1983 defense of teaching and integrity (*To Know As We Are Known*), considers one of a teacher's greatest gifts, "a capacity for connectedness." The challenge and the burden of the classroom became, in Palmer's choice words, "to weave a complex web of connection" between myself, my subject, my students, and eventually my community and my scholarship "so that students can learn to weave a world for themselves. . . . The connections made by [such] teachers," Palmer wisely notes, "are not held in their methods but in their hearts— meaning heart in its ancient sense, as the place where intellect and emotion and spirit and will converge in the human self" (xix).

These two guiding forces—the call of institutional citizenship and an integrative impulse that forms the moral gravity of my world view—have become the latitude and longitude of my current working life. As such, they have brought me into the national service-learning movement and the practice of public scholarship while forcing me to question and reevaluate my place in the contemporary humanities.

The passion for convergence, I should briefly explain, sets me at odds against a new generation of academics who have redefined the humanities agenda. While many academic fields—physics is the obvious example—are striving toward a vocabulary of disciplinary consilience, most humanities disciplines have taken a sharp opposite turn into postmodernism. Especially attractive are its explicit prohibitions against universal truths, its skepticism over all claims for connectivity and consensus, and its rejection of an Enlightenment discourse of "spirit," "heart," "will," and "human self"—a vocabulary, as one of my young colleagues gently put it, that "reeks of the rotting carcass of liberal humanism." The strong ideological position staked out in new humanities fields like cultural studies, bolstered by curriculum reforms inspired by hard-line multiculturalism, are heavily freighted with postmodern skepticism over the possibilities for integration, unification, consilience, and the "public sphere." Bemoaning the hard inward turn of scholarship and postmodernism's "spectatorial approach" to the public arena, Richard Rorty warns in a lecture on "A Cultural Left" published in *Achieving Our Country* (1998): "to step into the intellectual world which [postmodernists] inhabit is to move out of a world in which the citizens of a democracy can join forces to resist sadism and selfishness into a Gothic world in which democratic politics has become a farce" (95). I was drawn to the possibilities of public scholarship at a time when critical and theoretical underpinnings among new humanists were premised on liberation from suffocating notions of "public," "common" knowledge, and "common" truths—all routinely disparaged as oppressive grand narratives and dismissed as archaic cartoons and pernicious fantasies.

For many of my younger colleagues, in particular, the democratic ties that bind individual lives to the common welfare are now viewed, through the skeptical lens of postmodernism, as political shackles that oppress. A shared body of moral values that integrates a curriculum into a social order threatens to become, we are warned, a pretense for domination by privileged classes and groups. Moreover, an interdisciplinary curriculum that aims for balance, commonality, and synthesis, according to postmodern pedagogy, is really no different than a curriculum that seeks to eradicate differences, thereby reinforcing ethnocentrism, cultural hegemony, and class oppression.

Just at the same time, then, as my own academic work and teaching life broke through into a new set of commitments to transcend difference and seek common ground with others, my humanities colleagues were becoming far less concerned with the spirit of integration. They were much more preoccupied with ideology, identity politics, power, and the anxieties and turf skirmishes of the academic culture wars. Having emerged from the throes of personal crisis and professional divisions, I was bent on nourishing the fragile bond between the inner life and ethical responsibility to work, institution, and community—the essence, I believe, of a humanities education. Meanwhile, the disciplinary venue where I was situated to carry out my new work had become mental, abstract, contentious, and theory-driven.

In many ways my beef with the contemporary humanities reinvigorated some long-held commitments with important questions. How, for example, could I renew my own writing with the capacities and qualities of humanistic inquiry that I profess theoretically and defend in the abstract? How could I teach and write with moral clarity, integrity, authenticity, and heart in an intellectual climate that had become much too cerebral, too much *in the head?* Where could I find a community of fellow practitioners for whom the inner life, ethical commitment, and generative responsibility are central to career and not objects of derision or signs of philosophical bad faith? How could I find my way to common work in the university with its intellectual climate clouded by suspicion over consensus, commonality, and community?

Such questions compelled me to conduct wide-ranging examinations of civic and democratic purpose as they relate to curriculum, scholarship, and my own sense of self-purpose as a member of my community and university. I emerged from my season of professional disappointments with a renewed generative commitment and a greater capacity and need to build connections with others. I was also looking for ways to integrate what struck me as an artificial and even hypocritical division of academic life into the separate boxes of scholarship, teaching, and service. I was especially eager to explore avenues of service and find ways of becoming a participant in community and not, as I had been virtually my whole life, a spectator and critic quick to point out the failings and shortcomings of social life from my self-imposed vantage point, safely on the societal fringes. In addition to suiting up for community life, I wanted to integrate practices of service back into teaching and scholarship. Like many academics, however, I lacked a vehicle through which I could transform my teaching and scholarship into concrete expressions of social and moral action. *How could I be of service?* Now that I had gained a foothold on career security, I also lacked a model I could apply to integrate the professional pathways of teaching, research, and service. I found that vehicle and that model in service-learning pedagogy and philosophy, in a socially engaged scholarship, and in civic partnerships and community-based learning and research practices that I easily recycled back into the challenges and rewards of curriculum development work and program building.

First, I parlayed the precious franchise of tenure into an assignment as editorial consultant to the Center for Urban Affairs at my university. The outreach scholarship practiced by urbanists, public policy analysts, community activists, and graduate students pursuing degrees in community and economic development offered me new outlets and opened new intellectual horizons. I began experimenting with a public scholarship and a language of engagement that countered the theoretical and self-referential turn of work in my home College of Arts and Letters. Land-grant historian Scott Peters, for example, offers a simple litmus test of "how a scholar's work of constructing and communicating knowledge might contribute to community-building, to public problem solving, to public creation, and to the process of coming to public judgment on what ought to be done . . . to address important public issues and problems" (1996, 32). David Brown speaks of "'interrogating practices' that help citizens break through the proprietary languages of academics so that their specialized vocabularies can be made intelligible, be reflected on, and used without license by nonspecialists" (1995, 40).

Gradually, a wealth of new opportunities presented themselves where I could ply my modest talents as an editor, teacher, and writer and practice a nontechnical prose accessible to the world outside the academy. I designed, for example, a practicum for graduate students interested in applying public literacies to their theoretical and quantitative fields. I edited the proceedings of a statewide summit meeting on the future of Michigan cities sponsored by the Michigan House of Representatives' Bi-partisan Urban Caucus. I helped plan the programs for Summer Institutes offered to community-based organizations and local nonprofits on such topics as closing the digital divide and creating sustainable communities. I wrote public policy briefs. I created opportunities for English majors to work as staff writers for community outreach units that specialized in youth and families, minority empowerment, education, and health and human services. Given my new working relationships with community partners, it was an easy and logical step to design and implement a general-education writing program back in my home department that featured community-based writing placements and a curriculum that centered on civic life and writing in the public interest. I joined with a colleague and we published a comprehensive curriculum development resource guide for other writing teachers that included theoretical, historical, and rhetorical analyses along with practical tools and a portfolio of sample student projects. With a diverse group of colleagues from across the country, I took part in a research work group for five years, sponsored by the Kettering Foundation, on democracy and deliberation in higher education. Community-based learning and research, in short, fulfilled my continued longing for relevant public work. Moreover, my own research agenda was energized by the fresh enthusiasm I had for a socially engaged scholarship. I brought renewed interest, for example, to the strand of democratic humanism that runs through American civic life from Tocqueville to Martin Luther King Jr. I examined the Settlement House movement and civil-rights era Citizenship Schools as historic hubs of civic education and applied humanities. I published articles on public philosophy, moral and civic literacy, rhetoric and public discourse. I wrote essays for more popular venues on liberal education, engaging young people in democratic practices, and the humanities and public life. Old voices spoke anew—Jane Addams, Walt Whitman, John Dewey, Langston Hughes.

In short, I found a way to pick up the gauntlet Ernest Boyer threw down in *Scholarship Reconsidered* (1997, 3): "Can America's colleges and universities, with all the richness of their resources, be of greater service to the nation and the world? Can we define a scholarship in ways that respond more adequately to the urgent new realities both within the academy and beyond?" I entered as fully as I could into the public dimensions of the humanities. I believed for the first time in years that the humanities could play a public role envisioned by Jane Addams at Hull House: as a means of inviting citizens to be interpreters of their own lives while bringing critical resources like analysis, reflection, deliberation, and ethical action to bear on social and cultural renewal. At the same time, I underwent a more introspective sounding of my own moral life. I came to terms with questions that had vexed me. How can I redirect my scholarship into a life of meaningful service? Or refashion my service into reputable scholarship? And transform my teaching into both?

At the risk of overstatement, I have to say that community-responsive teaching initiatives and my gradual retooling as a public scholar made me *whole.* They provided a parallax, as Robert Frost puts it, to "unite / My avocation and my vocation / As my two eyes make one in sight." They gave me a kind of template for professional integration just when I needed it to kick-start a career marked by enough conflict, separation, division, suspicion, and isolation. I was able to find a way to act on the integrative drives that accompanied my professional reprieve. Public scholarship and service learning put Humpty Dumpty back together again by converging the separate pathways of scholarship, teaching, and professional service into the thoroughfare of an integrated professional and personal life.

That convergence calls me back to the late 1970s and my stint as an itinerant composition teacher crisscrossing Providence on a bus, making connections—literally—between such seemingly disconnected classrooms, neighborhoods, and institutional missions. Crouched in the high anxieties of career uncertainty, I knew then—faintly, tentatively, quizzically—that this is what I really desired: the ethical life of service, intellectual stretch and challenge, and the call to moral duty. Twenty-five years later I find myself on a bus ride with tenure, a witness to T. S. Eliot's culminating wisdom in the *Four Quartets*:

> We shall not cease from exploration
> And the end of all our exploring

Will be to arrive where we started
And know the place for the first time.

REFERENCES

Boyer Ernest. 1997. *Scholarship Reconsidered: Priorities of the Professoriate.* Princeton, NJ: Carnegie Foundation for the Advancement of Teaching; San Francisco: Jossey-Bass.

Brown, David. 1995. "The Public/Academic Disconnect." *Higher Education Exchange*, January: 38–42.

Elshtain, Jean Bethke. 1995. *Democracy on Trial.* New York: Basic Books.

Erikson, Erik. 1968. *Identity: Youth and Crisis.* New York: Norton.

Lasch, Christopher. 1995. *The Revolt of the Elites and the Betrayal of Democracy.* New York: Norton.

Palmer, Parker. 1983. *To Know As We Are Known: Education as a Spiritual Journey.* San Francisco: Harper and Rowe.

Peters, Scott. 1996. "The Civic Mission Question in Land Grant Education." *Higher Education Exchange*, January: 25–37.

Rorty, Richard. 1998. *Achieving Our Country: Leftist Thought in Twentieth-Century America.* Cambridge: Harvard University Press.

EDUCATION FOR DEMOCRACY:

A CONVERSATION IN

TWO KEYS (2004)

A Note to Readers
In March 2001, a diverse group of thirty-three juniors and seniors
representing twenty-seven colleges and universities gathered at the Johnson
Foundation in Racine, Wisconsin, for the Wingspread Summit on Student
Civic Engagement, sponsored by Campus Compact. Nominated by faculty
and community service directors, the students participated in candid
group discussions focused on their generation's "civic experiences" in higher
education.

The New Student Politics: The Wingspread Statement on Student
Civic Engagement, *written by Sarah E. Long, then an undergraduate*
at Providence College, describes the Wingspread students' thinking and
reports on their practices of political and civic involvement, politics,
and service. The Statement *provides specific suggestions about how*
campuses can improve their commitment to student civic engagement
through service learning, increased support for student political activity,
better attentiveness to student voice, and the development of more
relevant frameworks for student participation in the political process.
The Statement *also captures the tensions and promise surrounding*

meanings the Wingspread students assign to politics, education, and their development as citizens. (Readers can access The New Student Politics *through the Campus Compact website.)*

In the following essay, first delivered as a keynote address, I intersperse a commentary on The New Student Politics *with quotes, set in bold, adapted from the* Statement. *I don't intend the excerpts to be treated as conventional block quotes used to embelish my own text. Rather, they are dropped into strategic moments of my argument as stand-alone pull quotes. During the original keynote, I asked an undergraduate to read the excerpts in an effort to get the voice right. The result is a "conversation in two keys"—a deliberative and reflective dialogue between two generations searching for a common chord to carry on the shared work of democratic citizenship.*

By the time my students read *The New Student Politics* they weren't in much of a mood, it seemed to me, to parse and sort through its arguments. Earlier in the semester, they had already been actively involved in public work. They had felt something of the promise of political engagement through public interest research and public literacy projects that brought them into direct contact with senators and representatives at the state capitol. A centerpiece of the course was, in effect, a classic lobbying campaign. Students designed, refined, and carried out strategies to distribute among key state legislators a booklet on youth public policy perspectives—*Generation Y Speaks Out: Public Policy Perspectives through Service-Learning*—researched, written, and produced by two previous classes. Our goals were twofold. First, get *Gen Y* into the hands of influential shapers of public policy. Second, present persuasive arguments to those policy shapers that the student voices in *Gen Y*—and the voices of their generation at large—deserve a place in the deliberation and implementation of public policy in Michigan. As one of the original student authors, quoted in a press release drafted by my students, said: "Older generations think we're slackers, but this type of project shows that we really do care and want to make a difference. Our ultimate goal is to change a law or influence policy in some way. Then we'd know that our voice is really being heard." In the course of their projects, my students testified before legislative commit-tees, met with house and senate staffers, designed PowerPoint pitches, wrote letters, e-mails, executive summaries, press releases, and so on. Along the way they studied *A Citizen's Guide to State Government* and *The Legislative Process in Michigan: A Student's Guide*. Meanwhile, students had plenty of opportunity to read, write about, and reflect upon the rap, made by Robert Putnam in the influential *Bowling Alone* (2000) and others (whom we read), that their generation was doing more than its part to continue a legacy of disinvestment in our country's social capital.

> **We discovered at Wingspread a common sense that while we are disillusioned with conventional politics (and therefore most forms of political activity), we are deeply involved in civic issues through non-traditional forms of engagement. We are neither apathetic nor disengaged. In fact, what many perceive as disengagement may actually be conscious choice.**

By stirring *The New Student Politics* into this learning mix, I thought its self-drawn portrait of a generation deeply committed to political life through nontraditional practices of civic engagement would be catalytic and energizing—adding light, weight, depth, and complexity to our sub-ject, "Public Life in America." I hoped too that the statement would hasten deeper reflection on the role young people can play in shaping public policy closer to home in Michigan. But instead of galvanizing further critical con-versation and reflection, our discussions of *The New Student Politics* just plugged along in fits and starts. I had a heck of a time trying to find some decent wind so I could plot a course through the *Statement*. About the only thing that sprung us from the doldrums was my students' interest in testing a claim made by their Wingspread peers. Do the schools they attend, my students wondered, live up to the charge that colleges and universities must do a better job of offering students more "ways to deepen service-learning and enhance its capacity to promote civic engagement" ? The liveliest and most thoughtful critical discussions we had came from research my students did showing that the Wingspread students' home campuses (including our own), in some cases, had a lot of work to do to live up to that claim, especially the full integration of service-learning practices into general-education curricula, majors, and professional degree programs.

> **A number of universities, we agreed at Wingspread, appear to promote service and community outreach as ways to make themselves appear involved but do not seem interested in any real commitment to the outlying community. They seem to view service more as a public relations strategy, while, in reality, they keep the community at arm's length.**

What accounted for my students' lukewarm reception of *The New Student Politics*? Were they just fed up with another round of arguments—no matter what the source—about how their generation should find its way onto the public commons and learn to wield, in the words of one of the Wingspread students, the "hammer and chisel" of democratic citizenship?

Or had my students' involvement with conventional practices of civic expression, I wonder, left them ill-prepared for the alternative of "service politics" spelled out in the statement?

> **The Wingspread dialogues defined a form of political engagement we have chosen to call "service politics." Service politics is the bridge between community service and conventional politics. At Wingspread we argued that service is alternative politics, not an alternative to politics. Participation in community service is a form of unconventional political activity that can lead to social change, in which participants primarily work outside of governmental institutions; service politics becomes the means through which students can move from community service to political engagement. Those who develop connections to larger systemic issues building on their roots in community service adopt a framework through which service politics leads to greater social change.**

Do the civic skills the Wingspread students learn from service opportunities in their local communities differ from or maybe diminish or indeed eclipse those more mainstream skills my own students acquired from drafting public policy briefs, attending legislative committee meetings, and lobbying their state representatives? Had I made a mistake of shifting the service component of the course from interpersonal networks of direct service to institutional practices of organized political participation? Did that weaken or undermine the notion of "service politics" that the Wingspread students see as "the bridge between community service and conventional politics"? Maybe my biggest fear is that I unknowingly initiated my students into those kinds of conventional political activities that the Wingspread students are disillusioned with. As a consequence, had my students and I ended up practicing democracy less in terms of the Wingspread emphasis on the social responsibility of the individual and more in terms of the retrograde civic obligations of the citizenry? If so, no wonder my students, mired in the status quo of conventional politics, didn't catch fire from the statement's call "to pursue change in a democratic society."

These are important questions about pedagogy, disciplinary practices, institutional integrity, politics, history, and intergenerational sociology. They are questions about commitment and my students' identity and my own (shaky) self-image as a teacher, a service-learning practitioner, a member of my university community, and a player in the democratic life of my community and my country. These are also questions for the service-learning movement. They point to the difficulties and challenges of cross-fertilizing traditions of "service" to local communities and the latest clarion call for "civic engagement"—a coupling that seems so natural in a statement like *The New Student Politics* and on the letterhead of the Campus Compact. Meanwhile, practitioner faculty and their students and our brethren in student affairs along with our community partners sometimes struggle to get it right.

This class was the latest in a series of experiments begun in 1995 when several colleagues and I organized the Service Learning Writing Project

(SLWP), a research-intensive curriculum development initiative in service-learning and composition studies. We eventually established a new writing course—Public Life in America—that fulfills a general-education writing requirement and currently enrolls nearly 250 students a year in twelve stand-alone sections. Lately, our interests have turned to the relationship between rhetoric and democratic practices and the uses of deliberative democracy techniques for teaching writing and critical thinking—in particular, public forums and community-based study circles. Those are natural and intellectually fertile connections for many of us at a land-grant university teaching in a department with a strong American Studies tradition along with responsibilities for staffing required composition courses for over 6,000 freshmen a year and overseeing an undergraduate, masters, and Ph.D. program in rhetoric and professional writing with an emphasis on public culture studies, rhetoric, and community literacy. While SLWP courses vary widely in content and community partnerships, we all agree that argument, deliberation, and active participation in public life are essential ingredients of democracy and civic literacy. Our classes also share a commitment to principles of active and collaborative learning as well as public creation. For democracy to work, we stress to our students, ordinary citizens must take part in the process of identifying social problems, talking constructively about such problems, and finding solutions together. Much of the burden of reading, critical reflection, and discussion in our classes focuses on the troubling fact that too many citizens today—especially and most obviously young people—are not joining in the ongoing public work of democracy.

Running contrary, perhaps, to the argument in *The New Student Politics* that such disengagement is a conscious choice driven by frustration with conventional politics, my colleagues and I tend to assume that students' disengagement is *not* the flip side of an alternative politics but rather a direct expression of cynicism, apathy, indifference, or a sense of powerlessness.

At Wingspread, students expressed frustration about the derogatory ways in which they are often characterized by college and university presidents, faculty, and the public regarding their

> levels of political and civic engagement. Our contention is that,
> in fact, we are politically engaged, although we may participate
> in politics in unconventional ways.

One of the challenges I've taken away from the Wingspread students is that the moral claims informing the SLWP's public literacy curriculum may be sincere but misdirected. We might be asking the wrong questions: Why have we withdrawn from public association? Why does our democratic system—the putative envy of the rest of the world—seem to be failing us? Why have so many Americans lost faith in our common life? Instead, maybe we should be asking questions extrapolated from assertions made in the Wingspread statement. For example, how can we deepen our students' connections to the community through the kinds of experiences that move them from an awareness of issues into problem-solving strategies? What forms of civic engagements best fit our students' *personal* motivations to get involved—especially their anger, their hope, and the pragmatism they bring to the work of pursuing systemic social change? "Does the rhetoric of public service and being a good neighbor," as the Wingspread students themselves ask, "belie the realities that the students experience in the local community"—and, indeed, on their home campuses and *especially* in our classes? And what traditions in the life of our civic culture best sustain "service politics" as a catalyst for political engagement?

> One reason many of us choose to become involved in community
> service is that we dislike the institutional focus of conventional
> politics. We are frustrated with the workings of institutions,
> ranging from the federal government to our own colleges and
> universities. To many of us, developing real relationships with
> others through service is civic engagement. We at Wingspread
> associate affecting people with affecting the system.

If my presumptions of apathy and disengagement on the part of my students are indeed misdirected, I can take some small comfort from the fact that many others have made similar wrong turns. None of the serious studies that have seeded the widespread notion of the current generation's civic anemia have taken much account of the Wingspread students' new mantra of activism: "Community service is a form of alternative politics, not an alternative to politics."

The annual algorithms crunched by the UCLA Higher Education Research Institute's much-watched freshman survey, for example, chart a steady, predictable fifteen-year decline in student interest in conventional politics. The survey also reports that student volunteerism grew to record levels in the late 1990s, with nearly 72 percent of students reporting that they perform volunteer work and almost two-thirds agreeing that "helping others in difficulty" is an essential objective of their college life. But at no time has it occurred to the statisticians to *correlate* these ostensibly opposing trends into an expression of the Wingspread students' alternative configuration, "service politics." Instead, the pollsters question the validity of the 72 percent figure as a true marker of altruism, arguing that volunteer work looks good on student resumes—thereby reinforcing the caricature of today's college student as cynical and self-involved. No wonder the Wingspread students "reject many of the surveys, studies, and literature that have become the basis for a generalized portrait of young Americans, as this information often disregards local, relational, and unconventional forms of political/civic engagement."

In fairness to my good friends at UCLA, other oracular sources of generational insight are also called into question by "service politics" and the way it shifts democracy's center of gravity from political practices of civic obligation to moral expressions of individual social responsibility. Arthur Levine and Jeanette Cureton seem at a loss to explain a similar disconnect they found among 1990s college students between greater interest in community service and a significantly lower threshold of tolerance for the political arena. Their speculation, frankly, is a little thick. "Though fears and doubts about politics, politicians, and government are extremely high," they write in *When Fear and Hope Collide* (1998), "students have chosen to engage, albeit through the local and more informal approach of community service. In part, the reason stated for their involvement is that they had no choice; they had to embrace the political agenda or it would engulf them" (141).

Neil Howe and Bill Strauss, whose popular 1993 study, *13th Gen*, bristles with efflorescent cynicism, may get it only half right. In the "13th Gen," they speculate, "lies a reason for hope. As a group, they aren't what older people wish they were but rather what they themselves know they need to be: street-smart survivalists clued into the game of life the way it really gets played" (11). Hardbitten realists, in other words, instead of idealists bent on the difficult task, as the Wingspread students say, of achieving "an emerging identity that is not based on an idealized notion of the democratic citizen."

A similar disconnect shows up in the grim diagnosis conducted by Robert Putnam in his influential autopsy of the American body politic, *Bowling Alone*. Putnam relies upon the logic of "generational succession" to chart the steady erosion of social capital during the latter third of the twentieth century, all the way from the canary in the mineshaft of electoral politics to the current low levels of news and information literacy and sluggish grassroots political involvement. Each generation, according to that logic, accelerates the "treacherous rip current" of civic disengagement that scours civil society from our bowling alleys to our neighborhood polling precincts. Putnam's conclusion in his chapter on "Civic Participation": "Americans are playing virtually every aspect of the civic game less frequently today than we did two decades ago" when baby boomers came of age politically (41). By measuring civic engagement according to conventional political practices—petition signing, for example, or working for a political party and running for public office—and then aligning those practices to the boomer juggernaut, it's hard for an alternative expression like "service politics" to register on Putnam's sociological radar screen.

Some of us at Wingspread are critical of the fact that many surveys and literature on youth civic disengagement rely solely on conventional political activities—such as voting—as indicators of student political involvement. Students are not engaged in conventional political activities because conventional politics corresponds to an institutional system that we view as antiquated and irrelevant to our concerns and passions for social justice. We have turned away from political engagement and citizenship

rooted in institutions and systems in favor of civic engagement through local, community-based activities characterized as "community service" and other local, relational, and unconventional forms of political/civic engagement.

The irony, however, is that the Wingspread students' appreciation of the value of community service as a way to connect moral choices to larger social action is, by Putnam's own definition, a classic manifestation of social capital. The service experience, that is to say, evidences networks of mutual support, cooperation, trust, and even, in the form of service learning, institutional efficacy. But as an "alternative politics," service politics does not calibrate very well with correlations and frequencies generated by Roper polls. In his "Agenda for Social Capitalists" at the end of the book, Putnam acknowledges the value of school-based community service programs as good ways to exercise and strengthen "the civic muscles of participants" (405). Nonetheless, Putnam treats service learning, at best, as a bridge that will *lead to* greater student involvement in conventional forms of civic expression such as a return to 1960s levels of voter turnout. Putnam ends up reinforcing the notion of service as an alternative route to politics as usual, not an "alternative politics." He's stuck on a familiar binary: "service," like time in the weight room, is good preparation for the real "civic game."

This much is fairly clear: cynicism, skepticism, pessimism, and an outright rejection of politics-as-usual runs rampant among our students. But there's something that might not be so clear to the pollsters. Our students are not part of a generation that is civically *disengaged* or ethically disoriented. I am not a social scientist, but I suspect that sociological survey methodologies and quantitative analytical techniques don't do paradox very well. Nonetheless, it is impossible to avoid the paradoxical features of our students' civic profile. Findings from focus groups conducted by KRC Research for the Campus Compact's Student Civic Engagement Campaign show, in fact, that the very term "civic engagement"—broadly defined as "action designed to identify and address issues of public concern"—turns off most students. They "reject the idea [of civic engagement] as irrelevant to their current lives and unsuccessful at inspiring them to take future action." Still, especially among student leaders like those invited to the Wingspread gathering in March 2001, "it is apparent," the KRC "Findings" memorandum concludes, "that the level of civic engagement is strong" when measured by such things as "interpersonal connection," "immediate gratification," "local community activities," and "the translation of actions of the individual into positive change." The value of *The New Student Politics*, it seems to me, is that the Wingspread students articulate an important conceptual scheme—"service politics"—that transforms an apparent contradiction into an interesting and insightful paradox: *our students hate the* idea *of civic engagement but they welcome opportunities to become civically engaged.*

What do these paradoxes and ironies mean, then, for our teaching? For one thing, they may help explain my own students' lukewarm reception of *The New Student Politics*. When my students were busy pressing their cases in the corridors of the state capitol, they bristled with activity and energy. Our classroom hummed with the churn of learning. They shut down, for the most part, when I sought to connect that public work to canons of civic literacy and the social contract in America and when I tried to shore up their felt practices of citizenship with an intellectual fretwork of concepts, ideas, and critical readings. The same thing happened with study circles we later convened among senior citizens at a local community center. My students fussed and throbbed with nervous energy as we planned, practiced, and facilitated the study circles. They shuffled through the drill when I tried to leaven those community dialogues with critical reflections on traditions of deliberative democracy in America. Maybe they went through the same motions, then, when we called another time-out from engaged learning projects to discuss and explain and sort through the ideas in *The New Student Politics*, even though those ideas stressed the importance of democratic citizenship as a matter of "build[ing] relationships and connect[ing] with others in concerted action."

Students experience a curricular deficit on their campuses. We perceive our institutions as willing players in the message of deferral of civic responsibility. Higher education is complicit

**in compartmentalizing the public-civic life and the private-
economic life of students. This is illustrated in pedagogy that
requires us to live in bifurcated worlds of theory and action.
We are told to ingest large amounts of information that point
to a concern, yet we are often discouraged from action on our
knowledge and idealism until we have safely secured our own
economic futures.**

Beyond that, with the help of the Wingspread students (although I'm
not sure they would want to claim the credit) I am beginning to sense a shift
in the sorts of teaching challenges we face as the service-learning movement
evolves into the "civic engagement campaign." The old challenge to deeply
integrate students' experiences in their community service placements with
course content is giving way to the new challenge, put simply, of manag-
ing the rupture or the disconnect between action and ideas that, for better
or worse, characterizes our students' predominant learning style and their
modus operandi as citizens. While the old challenge was pedagogical, the
new challenge, it seems to me, is largely epistemological. Levine and Cureton offer good insight into this disconnect in their analysis of "the widening
gap between the ways in which students learn best and the ways in which
faculty teach" (128). Citing research done at the University of Missouri–
Columbia, they note that

> today's students perform best in a learning situation characterized by
> "direct, concrete experience, moderate-to-high degrees of structure, and
> a linear approach to learning. They value the practical and the immedi-
> ate, and the focus of their perception is primarily on the physical world."
> Three-quarters of faculty, on the other hand, "prefer the global to the
> particular, are stimulated by the realm of concepts, ideas, and abstrac-
> tions, and assume that students, like themselves, need a high degree of
> autonomy in their work." In short, students are more likely to prefer
> concrete subjects and active methods of learning. By contrast, faculty are
> predisposed to abstract subjects and passive learning. (128)

Such a mismatch of learning styles, teaching practices, and knowledge claims is especially acute—and its impact largely ignored—in the humanities. Marooned in the arcanum of postmodernism, the contemporary humanities are far more preoccupied with theories of social control and construction, ideology, power, cultural production, and the dynamics of social class than they are with the gritty proposition that students might ache to engage actual social and class issues as they play out in their own communities. Suffice it to say that too few literature students, for example, who are immersed in important ideas of racial and gender oppression in their English classes are required or invited by their professors to become civically engaged in those issues as they are lived out and suffered through in their own local communities.

> **Colleges have a significant role in helping students develop a public, social imagination. The Wingspread students suggest that colleges challenge them not by informing students of a set of civic duties, but by modeling for us the right way to be in a community, particularly how to subordinate individual desires to a larger public purpose—even while living in a market economy that defines success by the fulfillment of those individual desires.**

I cannot legitimately speak to the situation in the social and natural sciences, but it seems to me that the humanities must do a better job of bridging this gap the Wingspread students see on their campuses between a culture of ideas and a commitment to action. They witness that gap throughout the geography of their institutions. They recognize, for example, that "uncontested skepticism is welcomed in contemporary university culture as a sign of intellect" while they "long for ideals to believe in and for those 'idealists' who will inspire them." They take pride in "the larger activities and mission of [their campuses that] are aligned with the values of inclusion, justice, reciprocity, community building, and participatory democracy." Meanwhile, throughout their conversations in Racine "we concluded that the [university's] theoretic relationship with the community often differs from the real."

The Wingspread students yearn to make service a more widespread and integral part of the curriculum, yet they are understandably skeptical over the moral life of their own campuses. Colleges and universities, they write, "rarely provide models for healthy communities, either on campus itself (where the hierarchical nature of the institution often overlooks students needs/input when making decisions), or through relationships with the surrounding community." Finally, they frankly admit that service activities and public work are "rarely celebrated on par with academics" on campuses where administration and faculty encourage students "to be primarily consumers of knowledge and democracy—not active producers."

These insights spelled out in *The New Student Politics* underscore and advance, in our students' own words, four responses Elizabeth Hollander, Richard Cone, and I wrote about in 2001 as we considered ways to better engage and empower student voices and clear a path to civil society in our classrooms, and when we wondered whether faculty were up to the task. I don't think Liz and Dick would mind if I reiterated those responses here as both a coda to this brief commentary and as a way to reframe the key themes and contributions of *The New Student Politics* to the national civic engagement campaign.

First, we argued in an article in the March–April issue of *About Campus*, we must honestly encounter, on their own terms, our students' cynicism and self-involvement. This means we must empathize with and not resent our students' pessimism, ambivalence, and alienation from public life. Surprisingly, we have discovered the rap that today's young people are fatalistic and disengaged does not run very deep. Second, it is important to infuse our teaching practices with the spirit of democracy. We understand democracy not only as a set of political practices but, more importantly, as a body of moral commitments and ethical claims that inform the climate of values and techniques in our classrooms. Third, we have learned to teach on our feet, seizing on events in the community or nation that offer a teaching moment, even if it means scrapping a unit from a carefully designed syllabus. Lastly, we need to struggle to overcome the bias, deeply engrained in Western teaching practices, that a student's "inner life" and "public self" are separate spheres of moral development. On the contrary, they are intimately connected. In the words of Parker

Palmer from *The Courage To Teach* (1998), "only as we are in communion with ourselves can we find community with others" (92).

These same pedagogical principles, we went on to say, can be applied to the campus as a whole. How often do our campuses model the "spirit of democracy" in how decisions are debated and made? How much opportunity do we provide for students to explain the sources of their distance from public life? How much do we integrate thinking about students' inner lives and public selves?

Administrators and others in higher education often dismiss student voice. Instead, we are encouraged to be primarily consumers of knowledge and democracy—not active producers. This sends the negative message that our contributions to knowledge, as well as the very tenets of democracy, are unimportant or misguided. What became evident during the Wingspread Summit was that students want to be in conversation with college presidents and other administrators and not treated as "fine china" brought out to impress trustees and honored guests.

On a more private note, the Wingspread students have emboldened me to a claim I've made so many times in the last few years that I sometimes worry it might lose its critical edge and moral force. They remind me that listening to student voices and bringing students into a meaningful and productive relationship with civic life are particular and problematic challenges for today's faculty. We humanists, in particular, are drawn to a compelling but competing notion—sanctioned, in part, by the triumph of theory over praxis and, in part, by the cult of meritocracy and specialization we have bought into—that the university and its airy world of ideas is a place apart from the friction, heat, and hurly-burly of the public sphere. This is not the first time I've been left with an unflattering realization coming off the heels of an exercise in generational humility. Maybe if we boomers just got out of their way, our students could realize the potential of their civic involvement. Those of them gathered at the Wingspread Summit on Student Civic

Engagement, in any event, "think time may prove that ours is one of the most politically active generations in recent history."

I hope so. I wish them well.

REFERENCES

Howe, Neil, and Bill Strauss. 1993. *13ᵗʰ Gen: Abort, Retry, Ignore, Fail?* New York: Vintage Books.

Levine, Arthur, and Jeanette S. Cureton. 1998. *When Fear and Hope Collide: A Portrait of Today's College Student.* San Francisco: Jossey-Bass.

Palmer, Parker J. 1998. *The Courage to Teach: Exploring the Inner Landscape of a Teacher's Life.* San Francisco: Jossey-Bass.

Putnam, Robert D. 2000. *Bowling Alone: The Collapse and Revival of American Community.* New York: Simon and Schuster.

IS CIVIC DISCOURSE

STILL ALIVE? (2007)

BEFORE STEPPING INTO THE TRICKY QUESTION OF CIVIC DISCOURSE'S current vital signs, it may be useful to consider a definition and a distinction.

First, what *is* civic discourse? "The whole purpose of democracy," Woodrow Wilson reminds us, "is that we may hold counsel with one another." Simply put, civic discourse is that mode of collective democratic counsel. It is the way citizens think about, form, and articulate their relations with public issues. Civic discourse happens through speech acts that span all sorts of rhetorical forms and practices, from diatribe and polemic to argument, debate, deliberation, and, not the least as we shall see, ordinary face-to-face conversation and personal narrative. I like to think of civic discourse as the rhetorical fretwork of democracy. It has to be strong enough to support and preserve the durable footings of democratic dissent—assembly, free speech, petitions of grievance. Its joints need to be flexible enough to accommodate changing climates, new voices, and new modes of communication such as digital environments and global information networks. And yet the framework needs enough human scale and respect for vernacular to sustain democracy as local, intimate, and interpersonal. From the local Revolutionary-era Committees of Correspondence that fed information to "a body Politick" hungry for information about political independence to recent Democracy Labs that propagate civic networks throughout cyberspace, modes of civic discourse enable citizens to answer the timeless and urgent call of democracy. As David Mathews and Nöelle McAfee put it in *Making Choices Together:* "We have a problem. We need to talk about it" (2000, 5).

I would urge, second, a capacious view of civic discourse, one that breaks down the convenient yet somewhat misleading distinctions we tend to enforce between *civil* behavior in the public sphere and the inevitable and welcomed agitations of *civic* exchange and churn in a healthy democracy. We also need to be wary and critically questioning of the way the mass media, in particular, tends to conflate civil behavior and civic speech in an otherwise understandable effort to truncate complex exchanges over public policy issues. The civic engagement movement that is sweeping through our high schools and colleges, for example, tends to treat *guidelines* for civil behavior—show respect for others, use a civil tone of voice, be courteous, weigh different points of view equally—as interchangeable with *practices* of civic dialogue: for example, making tough choices over controversial issues that people care passionately about, aggressively countering misinformation, recognizing that divisions exist within communities and not glossing over them, and respecting that consensus-making brings *felt* personal sacrifices to some citizens.

A recent incident at my own university may help clarify what I mean. A coalition of conservative student groups invited to campus the founder of a radical grassroots citizens organization based in the Southwest that opposes current U.S. immigration policy. The organization sponsors citizen patrols along the border aimed at stemming illegal immigration from Mexico. A campus Chicano/Latino student group vigorously opposed the invitation. They showed up at the lecture and shouted down the speaker as implacably racist and anti-immigrant. Five students were handcuffed by campus police, removed from the lecture hall, and subsequently arrested. The press treated the story as a boilerplate incident of uncivil behavior on the part of the students that violated the speaker's free speech rights, when in fact the arrest of the five students and the presence on campus of the controversial speaker were only the nodal points of a civic energy that shot across campus and went completely unnoticed by the press. That energy prompted conversations about immigration, diversity, family and town histories, and the roles and responsibilities of higher education in a democracy that rippled through our campus, from the president's office and the newsroom at the student paper to dormitory cafeterias and sorority lounges. It provided a backstory that many faculty used as a learning moment in classrooms across campus. My point in raising the incident: we need to be careful to not mistake the polar extremes of publicized behaviors for the vast landscape of civic life that percolates between them. John Adams recognized this distinction when he urged colonists not to mistake the "Heats and Convulsions" occasioned by the tempers of revolution for the hard work of nation building taking place "in Assemblies, Conventions, Committees of Safety and Inspection, in Town and County Meetings [across] every Colony of the 13" (Rakove 1979, 101). Neither should we mistake the uncivil behavior of the Chicano/Latino students and the boorish self-satisfaction of their conservative peers as canaries in the mineshaft of our civic life. It is true that the organizing polarities defining civic America are growing further apart. I do not see this necessarily as a worrisome sign. On the contrary, the middle landscape of civic activity and democratic churn—what Walt Whitman celebrated as America's vast Democratic Vistas—is constantly expanding across new frontiers, new ethnic configurations, new discourse practices, and new opportunities for investment of social capital, including the blogosphere and the proliferation of chatrooms and listserves where citizens today exercise what Harry Boyte calls "civic muscle" while practicing the aerobic activity of democracy.

Back to our lead question: "Is civic discourse still alive?" The question carries a premise that hints at its own answer. Once vibrant and virile, civic discourse is now on the ropes, or near them, maybe even down for the count. The real answer, of course, is far more complex, uncertain, problematic, and, for what it implies about the health of our democracy, much more challenging. The public sphere—the marketplace of civic discourses in a democracy—is neither a boxing ring nor a place of perfect harmony or dependable consensus-building. Instead, public culture is pulled between these extremes, while language practices tend to obey the historical, political, and social forces that set public culture in motion. At any one moment in time it may seem as though civic discourse ebbs strongly—pulled by the tidal action, for example, of a nation's recovery from the shared traumas of war, economic depression, natural disaster, and dislocation—or wanes precipitously, following the active fault lines of national divisions, ideological inertia, partisan gridlock, and exhausted social capital. I offer here a view of civic discourse that oscillates between these extremes, one that both encourages consensus-building and deliberative action and tolerates conflict, argument, and sharp elbows.

What is particularly striking about the state of civic discourse in America today is the narrative extremes it accommodates. As I write (early April 2007), for example, every news cast—including the venerable *NewsHour*, the predicable network news programs, and the rough-and-tumble cable news shows—features a clip from Fox News' *The O'Reilly Factor* where host Bill O'Reilly and guest Geraldo Rivera nearly come to blows over the issue of immigration. Triggered by a recent incident in Virginia involving an undocumented drunk driver, the exchange quickly descends from virulent debate into blood sport theater. It's like witnessing a street fight or a car crash: you want to turn away but you can't. Meanwhile, almost simultaneously to O'Reilly and Geraldo's dueling rants, 500,000 people rally in Washington, DC, for a National Day of Action for Immigration Justice intended to urge compromise on immigration reform legislation pending before Congress. Organized by the National Capital Immigration Coalition (NCIC), the peaceful march is barely mentioned on television news. The tone of the rally is intentionally positive. Banners stress messages of justice and reconciliation. Speeches focus on strengths of the immigrant community and the shared immigrant experience as a source of common American identity. Meanwhile, elsewhere, silently folded into the national conversation over immigration policy—and mentioned nowhere in national news broadcasts—hundreds of public meetings organized by the National Issues Forum are taking place in communities across America. Citizens have been deliberating "The New Challenges of American Immigration" for months in two-hour public forums in places like the Morris, Minnesota Senior Center, the Des Plaines, Illinois Public Library, and the Center for Civic Life at Franklin Pierce College in Rindge, New Hampshire. These small, local practices of democratic deliberation in which ordinary citizens join together to get a handle on the complex issue and public policy implications of immigration are completely ignored by national broadcast media and wire services.

O'Reilly and Geraldo's eight-second sound bite of spit and insult is endlessly replayed. The NCIC rally and the thousands of "We Are America" signs are barely noticed. The senior citizens in Morris, Minnesota, are hardly news. Fortunately, the vital signs of civic discourse do not follow the same laws as the proverbial query about whether a tree falling in the forest makes any sound if no one is around to listen. On the contrary, one can argue that the silence is deafening.

Recent studies suggest, in fact, that Americans are fed up with attack commentary and eager to talk about and reconcile issues that separate local communities and polarize national debate. We are in a mood to move from conflict to comity. In a speech to the National Civic League's 100th National Conference, Daniel Yankelovich reported, well before the galvanizing events of 9/11, that American public opinion continues to reflect a widespread desire "to reconcile new social mores with American core values," including "a sense of community, neighborliness, hope, [and] optimism" (1995, 15). That sentiment was confirmed by several national surveys conducted in the late 1990s. They showed that the fraying of social integuments worried a majority of Americans who want to conciliate individual and group differences in the interest of dispelling what many perceive as a malaise that had settled over the public sphere. In one survey, 80 percent of respondents agreed that more emphasis should be put on community-building even if it meant compromising the pursuit of self-interest and individualism Americans have always cherished (Putnam 2000, 25).

One of these studies was conducted by the Harwood Group for the Kettering Foundation. Researchers convened several focus groups around the country. They distilled from hundreds of stories a comprehensive report about how American citizens form relationships among themselves around various public problems and concerns, many of which—for example, deficit reduction, school reform, health care, international trade—are still relevant today. One overriding theme stressed throughout the report is that *conversation* plays a central role in the way citizens connect to public concerns. While we may *listen* to O'Reilly and Geraldo on the airwaves, *local dialogue* is the most valued currency in our economies of public decision-making. "It is through conversation," the Harwood Group researchers conclude, "that people learn from one another, that problem solving occurs, and that a sense of hope springs forth for the future" (1993, 2).

Briefly, nine factors emerged in the Harwood Group's conversations with citizens that can be used as a barometer to measure the climate of our civic discourse.

1. Citizens have a desire to make connections *between* public concerns, rather than isolating one issue from another.
2. People value personal context. It is the lens through which they view public concerns. Instead of defining personal context as pure self-interest, however, citizens typically draw on their life experiences, personal stories, and imagination to establish ties to public concerns, not as sources of retreat from those concerns.
3. People express a keen desire for coherence in understanding public problems. Rather than relying on mass media for balanced information, citizens typically view the explosion of fragmented information that crowds our television screens as contributing to incoherence and misunderstanding.
4. People insist that they need room for ambivalence in the public arena. The drive to take a position on an issue and stick to it undermines the listening and testing of ideas that citizens value.
5. People expressed a range of emotions about public life. Emotion emerges as a natural and vital part of people forming relationships with public concerns.

6. People highly prize authenticity as being a crucial filter through which they view public life. In particular, citizens reported that they were generally distrustful of the language of experts because that language too often fails to capture the meaning of people's lives and concerns.

7. People yearn for a greater sense of possibility in public life. They are in search of an abiding belief, a feeling that it is possible to make progress on intractable public problems and that they themselves can play a meaningful role in bringing about that progress.

8. Citizens frequently talk about individuals in their daily lives who serve as catalysts—the person down the street, the family member, or the friend who spur them to discuss and act on public concerns.

9. Finally, citizens refer to the effectiveness of mediating institutions that serve as places for people to come together and talk about, learn, and act on public concerns.

Is civic discourse still alive? In light of the Harwood Group's findings, perhaps a more fruitful question might be: Where can citizens find good opportunities to practice civic discourses and conduct the work of reasoning together? And how can our public institutions—schools, libraries, neighborhood centers, museums—better facilitate civic discourses?

REFERENCES

Mathews, David, and Noëlle McAfee. 2000. *Making Choices Together: The Power of Public Deliberation.* Dayton, OH: Kettering Foundation.

Meaningful Chaos: How People Form Relationships with Public Concerns. 1993. A Report Prepared for the Kettering Foundation by the Harwood Group. Dayton, OH: Kettering Foundation.

Putnam, Robert. 2000. *Bowling Alone: The Collapse and Revival of American Community.* New York: Simon and Schuster.

Rakove, Jack N. 1979. *The Beginnings of National Politics: An Interpretive History of the Continental Congress.* New York: Knopf.

Yankelovich, Daniel. November 1995. "Three Destructive Trends: Can They Be Reversed?" Speech to the National Civic League's 100th National Conference. Philadelphia, PA.

FOUR SEASONS OF

DELIBERATIVE LEARNING (2008)

From 2002 to 2005, I set out on a systematic journey to incor-porate deliberative democracy and deliberative learning practices into a sequence of three new courses I developed in an interdisciplinary depart-ment of rhetoric and American Studies. The courses covered a full gamut of undergraduate teaching assignments, from a general-education requirement to a senior capstone project. This essay is partly a description of some of the techniques I tried out along the way, partly a lab report on the outcomes of the experiments I conducted, and partly a travelogue about the highs and lows of the journey—the exhilarating discoveries I made, the company I kept, as well as the wrong turns I took and jams I got into.

Each of the experimental classes along that journey is distinguished by a pedagogy that cross-fertilizes active learning techniques, principally service learning, and deliberative democratic practices, such as public forums, study circles, and civic engagement opportunities for students. Taken as a whole, my journey shows, I hope, that the synergy between deliberation and active learning can energize the undergraduate humanities classroom at all levels, even the senior capstone. Moreover, I bring away from these travels two key, but by no means original, insights into the value of deliberation and the challenge, as Daniel Yankelovich puts it, of "making democracy work in a complex world" such as ours. Democracy itself, I rediscovered, is fundamentally a rhetorical art. And deliberation, the discursive engine of democracy, can be a powerful, compelling, even transformative pedagogy that challenges students and teachers alike to connect principles, ideas, and critical reflection—the usual and venerable fare of the humanities classroom—to the crucible of lived community problems in which ordinary citizens conduct the extraordinary work of citizenship.

SETTING OUT: A TOEHOLD IN GENERAL EDUCATION

In the late 1990s, several colleagues and I organized the Service Learning Writing Project, a curriculum development and research initiative in service learning and composition studies. By yoking together rigorous classroom writing instruction, critical readings in American civic culture, and real-world writing projects in community, municipal, and nonprofit agencies, we found that students developed more complex understandings of the crucial role of language and critical thinking skills in the work of social and political change. We eventually established a new writing course in 1999—Public Life in America—which fulfills a general-education writing requirement and currently enrolls nearly three hundred students a year in twelve stand-alone sections.[1]

During the last few years, inspired largely by my participation in a Kettering Foundation work group, my interest has turned to the relationship between rhetoric and democratic practices and, in particular, to how deliberative democracy techniques might be used for teaching, writing, and critical thinking. Through continuing conversations and alliances with my colleagues at Kettering, I learned that the best way to promote a robust democracy is to encourage public deliberation of controversial issues, foster strong communities, and help promote citizens' civic, rather than professional identities. In the case of our students and higher education, this meant that to strengthen what Harry Boyte calls America's "civic muscle" we had to practice deliberative democracy in our classrooms and on our campuses.

I began experimenting, then, with methods of connecting the rhetorical and critical thinking requirements of my university's general-education writing course with Kettering's traditions of deliberative democracy and with the particular methodology of public conversation and problem solving practiced in hundreds of National Issues Forums (NIF) taking place across the country.

All these strands came together in 2002 when my colleague Eric Fretz and I designed a pair of closely related experimental writing courses in the general-education sequence that would provide students with opportunities to study techniques of deliberation and to practice both public dialogue and public problem solving. These two courses were not team-taught in the traditional sense. Fretz was scheduled to teach a writing section with a focus on Race and Ethnicity, and I was assigned a Public Life in America class with a special emphasis on education and youth issues. We each designed our own syllabus, although there was a good deal of overlapping of required texts, learning strategies, and writing assignments.

Our classes incorporated three active learning components, which we designed to link the academic issues of the separate courses, foster a strong learning community between our classes and among our students, and practice democratic skills of deliberation, collaboration, and participation. The first component involved setting up a fairly traditional service experience for students, and the next two components required students from both of our classes to collaborate on organizing an NIF forum on youth violence open to the public and, later on, to moderate smaller deliberative study circles in class.

Students practiced public dialogue and public problem solving early in the semester by conducting in-class practice forums on topics like the future of affirmative action and the quality of public education. (In my class, students even framed and deliberated a class attendance policy.) We devised several writing assignments, often in consultation with students, that moved students away from typical arguments based on debate to arguments anchored in the looser soil of deliberation. Students also analyzed, evaluated, and presented arguments on topics of current concern to local audiences, an activity we called "grassroots democracy in action."

Next, students gained important insights into public problems through question-and-answer sessions with invited guests (including a circuit court judge) and by working and learning in community settings with a number of community partners, including several Neighborhood Network Centers located in Lansing.[2]

Our students then collaborated in a number of small teams to research, organize, and host the public forum on "Violent Kids: Can We Change the Trend?" Students designed and drafted a discussion guide for forum participants and worksheets and instructions for moderator assistants. Students also handed out and evaluated pre- and postforum questionnaires. They self-selected into committees that worked on timetables and deadlines for various stages of forum organization, communications, publicity, and background research on things like children's television, media violence, and effects of video games.

After the forum, one of the work groups assembled and organized all of the forum work from each project team into a comprehensive portfolio. Fretz and I drafted and circulated to all of our students an extensive portfolio assessment and evaluation memo that critically addressed the contribution of each work group—all of which led to a deliberation we had not anticipated.

Our students were generally ruffled by our C+ evaluation of the portfolio. The grade was assigned to each student, and it counted for a sizable portion of their final grades. We took advantage of our students' dissatisfaction and invited them to put together a small deliberative forum to take a closer look at the evaluation memo and to present point-by-point arguments in favor of a higher grade. A small student work group agreed to frame the issue and prepare three choices for deliberation. Another work group took responsibility for moderating the joint-class forum, another for postforum reflections, and so on.

To give a flavor of how our students thought through the issue and how well they had integrated the deliberative process into the learning ethos of the classes, here is the discussion guide they prepared:

Choice 1: The NIF forum collaborative grade of C+ is fair and equitable.

Prof. Fretz and Prof. Cooper's evaluation memo is thorough, well argued, and reasonable. While some students may nit-pick with details, overall the judgment is sound and the conclusions are justified. All the students in [each class] clearly knew well in advance that the forum work would be evaluated with a common grade. Sure, some students may have worked harder than others. But to insure the integrity and honesty of the forum project as an exercise in democracy and public life, students must be willing to accept the common grade.

Choice 2: Working groups that excelled deserve a better grade than C+. On the other hand, the evaluation memo suggests that other working groups may deserve less than a C+.

The working groups should be evaluated on a group-by-group basis. Prof. Fretz and Cooper should grade each group according to the arguments made in the separate committee sections of the evaluation memo. This grading procedure is ideal because it takes into consideration *both* collaborative work and individual effort. It is also more fair. The downside: all the work groups knew from the outset that the portfolio would be graded collaboratively. Is it ok to change that policy after the fact?

Choice 3: The common grade for the NIF forum work should be higher.

The evaluation memo grade is simply too low. Granted, the points are well argued. No one claims Prof. Fretz and Cooper are being overly unfair. However, the forum was hard work for *all* students. It took up almost a third of the course work. It was a successful public deliberation. The portfolio, measured by even the toughest standards, was an excellent piece of work. No one disputes these points. Prof. Fretz and Prof. Cooper need to raise the grade, and the class will accept without question the higher common grade.

Fretz and I were convincingly swayed by Choice 3, and we raised the common grade to a B.

After the public forum—and once the dust had settled from the mini-forum on grading—our students had an opportunity, during the last two weeks of class, to moderate study circle sessions on "Youth Issues, Youth Voices" and "Changing Faces, Changing Communities" based on material provided by the Study Circles Resource Center in Pomfret, Connecticut. Study circles are smaller and more intimate than the typical public forum, so they give students more opportunities to prepare for, actively engage in, and moderate public discussions. We required each student in our classes to moderate at least one study circle discussion. We felt it was important to provide even the most reticent of our students the chance to practice habits of deliberation such as critical listening, asking leading questions, generating and sustaining discussions, staying neutral, and leading groups toward consensus.

Afterthoughts

Reflecting on our experimental classes convinced Fretz and me that engaging in public work in higher education means including students and their interests into the work and life of the classroom—even, and perhaps most important, in decisions about the syllabus and calendar, how to use class time and space, writing assignments, and evaluations. In an organic classroom like ours, where teaching/learning techniques have to mesh with pedagogical philosophy, teaching in the traditional sense of disseminating knowledge and downloading students with information becomes transformed into a collaborative process in which professors and students work jointly toward a common goal.

We discovered that learning strategies that promote public work through deliberative pedagogy offer teachers rewards and fresh perspectives as well as posing difficult challenges. Organizing public forums, facilitating off campus community-based learning experiences, practicing deliberative strategies, and codesigning assignments with students thrust faculty into new, sometimes uncomfortable positions. No longer the "sage on the stage," teachers become facilitators and, in many ways, colearners with students—and coworkers, too. We no longer directed from the sidelines or articulated abstractions behind a podium. We found ourselves doing work right alongside our students.

As we became facilitators and colearners, we had to give up some expectations about what should happen in a college classroom. In the process, we found new ways of thinking about those questions that all of us in higher education ponder: Where does the learning take place? How can I ratchet up the learning curve? What do I want my students to take away with them? Through practicing democracy in the classroom, we are able to answer these questions in different and more interesting ways than we could have in a more traditional classroom setting. Students learned disciplinary knowledge (in this case, writing rhetorical arguments, thinking critically, connecting written argument to concrete public problem solving) through experience and practice. In addition, they began to experiment with ways of operating and effecting change in the public sphere.

For our part, we learned that the role of professor is both bigger and smaller than the ones articulated by the traditions and expectations of our academic disciplines. Our most challenging and prosaic role, for example, was that of project manager. We helped our students anticipate snags, identify community and university resources, solve problems, develop networking skills, and lay out efficient workflows—skills we felt were basic to the toolkit of citizenship. We also fetched envelopes and department letterhead, provided campus contacts to facilitate logistics for the forum, and arranged for the use of printers, fax machines, office phones, and computers.

For me, a striking and lasting consequence of adopting and adapting to a deliberative pedagogy was that I no longer considered myself a "teacher" in the conventional sense in which my colleagues understood, practiced, and peer reviewed the role. Rather, I became an architect of my students' learning experiences or maybe a midwife of their practices of becoming better writers and active citizens—or, perhaps more to the point, something like a forum moderator. In a public forum, successful deliberation is often inversely related to the visibility and presence—indeed, the knowledge and issue expertise—of the moderator. The same applies to a teacher in a deliberative classroom: you spend a great deal of creative intellectual energy listening to students and learning to get out of their way so they can take ownership of the subject, in the same way that forum participants must "own" an issue.

That fundamental role shift totally changed my experience of the writing classroom, from mundane matters like the physical arrangement of desks and the venues where learning takes place to epistemological underpinnings, ethical practices and boundaries, not to mention problematic relationships with more traditionally minded colleagues who felt that I was cutting my students too much slack. In the annual department review, one of my colleagues criticized me, for example, for comments repeated on several narrative evaluations from students that "it was like the students were teaching the class." In the future, obviously, I need to do a better job of articulating a philosophy of deliberative pedagogy so my colleagues can translate statements like that as observations of practice and not criticisms of my teaching style.

The deliberative pedagogy that we employed demands a great deal of preparation and planning, but at the same time requires spontaneity and flexibility—and a certain degree of uncertainty. Our students' learning experiences encompassed complex and interlocking community groups, constituencies, organizations, and several offices and units at my university. Grounded in multiple learning partnerships, action research, and real-world contexts, learning became a dynamic social process—emergent, messy, edgy, relational, sometimes inconclusive, occasionally (though not often) painful and confused, frequently full of entanglements, and always, I hope, challenging. I found myself constantly pushing the class to a point of agitation, churning, and controlled chaos because that was where the real learning took place—at that threshold where students became present in, and took ownership of, their own learning experience.

130

THROUGH THE GATEWAY INTO THE
PROFESSIONAL WRITING MAJOR

Shortly after my experiments with deliberative democracy and pedagogy in the general-education writing sequence, my department expanded its mission by offering a new undergraduate degree in professional writing. The major is designed to capitalize on and complement our teaching, research, and outreach strengths in rhetoric and American Studies. In addition to preparing students for careers in professional writing, the major lays solid foundations for graduate work in rhetoric, writing, technical writing, the teaching of writing, and the study of culture. From the outset, the Professional Writing Program has emphasized the organizational, disciplinary, and cultural contexts for writing. Students specialize in one of three advanced writing tracks: (1) technical writing and writing in digital environments, (2) professional editing and publishing, and (3) writing in cultures and communities.

I saw the new major as a good opportunity to take what I had learned about deliberative democracy and active learning techniques in the general-education writing sequence and apply it to upper division courses in the major. Along with several colleagues from the Service Learning Writing Project, I served as a consultant to the curriculum planning committee for the "writing in cultures and communities" track. I later designed and taught the first gateway course for that track, appropriately titled Writing in the Public Interest, in which students explored various forms of public writing and their roles in democracy and public culture.

In this course, drawing on the history of civic culture in America, I used examples that highlighted the power and possibility of collaborative decision making. I saw these examples as case studies of deliberative democracy in action. They ranged from turn-of-the-century women's literary clubs and the nineteenth-century Chautauqua movement and Lyceum system, to twentieth-century settlement houses, citizenship schools, and the contemporary National Issues Forums. The study of these historical foundations helped prepare students to practice rhetorical conventions for deliberating and arguing in a democratic community. One of the important goals of the new course was to understand how language shapes community and democratic practices, and how, in turn, social processes and democratic traditions influence language.

Public writing and active learning were once again intertwined. Students worked with numerous local nonprofits and public advocacy organizations, from the Sexual Assault Crisis Intervention Center to the Ronald McDonald House, and for each practiced its particular conventions of public writing. Students compiled portfolios that were designed to get them "thinking rhetorically" about the groups with which they worked. They collected and analyzed examples of public writing. Students wrote essays about which forms of discourse were best suited to an agency or organization's public agenda, what messages were being communicated, what positions advocated, and at which registers of the public sphere the messages were aimed (local, regional, national).

Our reading and discussion revealed different intellectual and conceptual frameworks for "writing in the public interest." We examined case studies of what are called "rhetorical situations" and how they are bound up in issues of public interest. A rhetorical situation is an occasion that compels constructive argument in the public sphere. Such arguments—the rhetorical basis, it should be noted, for a deliberative forum—always take place within a social or public context, and within communities that define the relationships between writers/speakers, readers/listeners, and issues of shared import and concern. We looked, for example, at the way the Columbine High School shootings in Littleton, Colorado (April 20, 1990), created a rhetorical situation concerning gun control and youth violence that rippled across the country. Or how Janet Jackson's "wardrobe malfunction" at the 2004 Super Bowl prompted a rhetorical situation about decency, moral values, and the limits and responsibilities of broadcast media—issues we are still brooding over today.

A centerpiece of the course involved a semester-long project and partnership with the Michigan Campus Compact and the Michigan House of Representatives' Civics Commission (MHCC), a bipartisan initiative dedicated to the proposition that the best way to teach civics is to engage students in the public work of the state legislature. My students researched and designed Web-based, deliberatively framed opinion polls for the commission, aimed at providing college students throughout the state with a new venue to learn about and express their opinions on legislative proposals that had some bearing on young adult issues—for example, public smoking bans, state control of universities, and tough new "zero tolerance" laws on drunk driving. In addition to posting polling questions, students framed alternative positions on the proposals, prepared comprehensive background information, and analyzed polling results distributed to Michigan legislators.

Students hammered out a uniform template that they used to organize each of the twelve polls we posted to the MHCC website. The template called, first, for neutral, unbiased *background* information on the proposed legislation. "Does this information," students asked, "help in allowing poll participants to make educated decisions?" Next, each poll was preceded by a *highlights* paragraph, which presented positions on the bill and included a discussion of trade-offs associated with each position. "Make sure," students wrote in the poll-preparation guidelines, "to incorporate all sides—i.e., negative and positive facts [*sic*] because this is the last bit of information given before casting a poll vote."

Here is a sample poll students wrote for a proposed Zero Tolerance Bill on underage drinking:

CAST YOUR VOTE Under the Michigan Liquor Control Code, should the state give a person under the age of 21, who registers *any* level of bodily alcohol content (BAC), a misdemeanor with penalties that include automatic driver's license sanctions (for second and subsequent violations) and the possibility of a fine, community service, and substance abuse screening (at the violator's own expense) and/or substance abuse prevention or treatment services?

1. No. If an underage person is not physically seen consuming alcohol, it is unfair to enforce the same punishment as someone who was physically seen drinking.

(continued)

2. Yes. Drinking underage should have the same consequences, regardless of whether people are physically seen drinking or not.

3. Yes. Underage drinking is illegal. Any Zero Tolerance law in Michigan should have no exceptions. A misdemeanor with these penalties is a very lenient punishment for underage drinking.

4. No. There should be some leeway with what a person under the age of 21 can have in their system, due to the fact that mouthwash contains alcohol, and accepting wine at church will make the BAC levels rise.

Notice the way that the polling project captures many of the basic rhetorical components of deliberation, including (1) the importance of naming issues in comprehensible public terms that my students' college-age peers could relate to, (2) recognizing that facts and information about the zero-tolerance issue are important as a basis of deciding what is good for and valuable to the broader commonweal, (3) making choices that carry consequences, and (4) viewing individual behavior through the lens of public policy. To the extent that this poll and the others issued an invitation to college students statewide to be part of a public conversation, they became productive exercises in democratic decision making—especially for a generation of students for whom the Internet has become a dominant and accepted medium of communication, connection, and information gathering. "Deliberation," David Mathews and Noëlle McAfee of the Kettering Foundation remind us in *Making Choices Together,* has "the power to get people to take the first step to civic involvement. Deliberation also links these people to one another, creating a public, which is a body of people joined together to deal with common problems" (2000, 3).

Afterthoughts

As with the general-education writing class, I wanted this course to include public creation, community action, and democratic decision making. I designed the course so my students and I, along with the MHCC, formed a purposeful learning community that *practiced* the subjects it was exploring. In fact, everything I learned in the general-education writing class about the learning practices of deliberative communities was reinforced and intensified—and often brought to my mind the well-known comment of Myles Horton, founder of the Highlander School, in his 1997 autobiography, *The Long Haul.* "When you believe in democracy," he said, "you provide a setting for education that is democratic" (68).

My second season of democratizing the classroom suggested, like the first, that the sort of democratic pedagogy Horton has in mind must operate at multiple levels. It means, first and foremost, linking students' academic learning with experiences of democracy building and public work, learning that is rigorously situated in lived contexts and grounded in action. It also means trying to infuse the strategies and principles of democratic deliberation into every reach and recess of learning that takes place in the course, including, in particular, my own role as an active, engaged learner and a democratic practitioner. As a consequence, whenever I conduct a self-assessment of my courses now, I hardly ever ask, "How well am I teaching?" The critical questions for me are, what am I learning? and *am I getting out of my students' way?*

DESTINATION: THE ELECTIVE SEMINAR

The semester following the gateway course in the professional writing major, I was scheduled for an upper division Special Topics elective seminar in the American Studies Program. I saw it as another opportunity to continue experimenting with deliberative democracy and pedagogy. I also wanted to tackle some related questions that have troubled me since graduate school, questions that have roiled the field of American studies for the past thirty years, hounded the American democratic experiment since its inception, and continue to challenge our practices of deliberation and public decision making. Those questions were bluntly posed to my generation of American studies scholars/teachers by Harold Isaacs in the closing chapter of his 1975 classic *The Idols of the Tribe: Group Identity and Political Change.* Confronting the ethnic conflicts and dilemmas emerging in 1970s America, Isaacs warned, "The underlying issue is still: Can human existence be made more human, and if so, how? . . . How can we live with our differences without, as always heretofore, being driven by them to tear each other limb from limb?" (128).

The Latin motto *E pluribus unum* ("One from many"), selected in 1776 for the Great Seal of the United States, has been a source of inspiration and pride and, especially in recent decades, a cause of shattering controversy in America. A central question that has long perplexed Americans and American studies is how—and *whether*—we should reconcile our many separate, communal, ethnic, and group identities with a shared identity we hold in common as Americans.

I called the elective seminar Civic America. In it we took a close look at concepts like pluralism, civic culture, social capital, and civil society; historical and social movements; and grassroots practices of American public life that seek to make the tension in our democracy between "the many and the one" creative and productive. Since service, public work, and citizen participation are key ingredients in nourishing civil society, interested students were invited to sign up for a volunteer placement in a local community service or municipal agency that would give them a firsthand look at the challenges of civic America. Students who selected that option kept a separate journal in which they connected field experiences to seminar readings and discussions, and vice versa.

As I had done in the course called Writing in the Public Interest in the Professional Writing Program, I again embedded a strong emphasis on deliberation into themes and concepts of Civic America that could stand entirely on their own in any American studies class. We began with a groundwork of readings and case studies that vividly sketched out vocabularies and dilemmas of civic culture. We examined a series of grassroots portraits of democracy in action drawn from video vignettes produced by *The American Promise* series, including successful efforts to reintroduce wolves into Yellowstone National Park over the objections of local cattle ranchers, agitations by students at Gallaudet University to lobby for a new deaf president, and organizing efforts among largely Hispanic low-income neighborhood activists in San Antonio, Texas, for relief from chronic flooding caused by seasonal rains. We also winced through several examples of civic dysfunction, including political corruption in a small town on the Texas border and the failure of the city council in San Jose, California, to find a way to recognize, reconcile, and appease embattled groups squabbling over the placement of heritage monuments in a public park. Additions to the intellectual fretwork of a strong and historically informed view of civic America and the problem of the one and the many included seminar meetings on familiar synoptic formulations of civic culture, including monoculture and cultural pluralism. And we spent two meetings on the contemporary debate over multiculturalism.

I asked the twelve students in the seminar to hammer out a joint statement on what we had learned from these concepts and case studies about the problems and possibilities of civic America. They came up with a laconic three-sentence paragraph titled "The 16 Cs of Civic America," which could easily serve as an abstract on the hopes and perils of democracy. "Civic America," they wrote, "is an arena or a churn of competing, complex, conflicting claims. It can lead to confrontation, controversy, commitment, and courage. It can collapse into corruption, dysfunction, cynicism, and crime. It can yield consensus, conversation, compromise, common welfare, coexistence, and community." (My observation that the statement contained nineteen Cs instead of sixteen didn't seem to matter too much to them.)

Practices of deliberation centered around two major seminar projects, which were held during the second half of the semester. Each presented a variation of the pull between the one and the many—in the first case, around the tensions that the presence of Mexican day laborers brought to a primarily white community; in the second case, around the possibility that declining public support for and rising costs of higher education might prevent many low-income youngsters from entering college and increasing their opportunities for economic success and social and political empowerment.

The first project involved the screening of and extensive discussion about *Farmingville*, a 2004 award-winning documentary by Carlos Sandoval and Catherine Tambini, who lived and worked for nearly a year in the Long Island town of Farmingville. "*Farmingville*," according to the trailer, "provides a complex, emotional portrait of an American town in rapid transition from a relatively homogenous community to a 21st century village." The film intimately and painfully chronicles divisions between townsfolk, a politically split city council, and an influx of Mexican day laborers, which come to a head in the brutal beatings of two day laborers.

Each student was responsible for facilitating a deliberative discussion of several questions I posed (adopting some from the *Farmingville* program guide) about the way the film treated some of the core concepts about civic America we had been studying. The questions ranged from the specific to the global. For example: "What spurs people to cross the line from words, feelings, or beliefs to acts of violence?" And: "What new insights, features, and/or questions does *Farmingville* reveal about our subject, Civic America? Or confirm? Or, indeed, contradict?"

I was especially careful to craft our discussion of the film's potent content around the deliberative parameters of a public forum, and I borrowed techniques of facilitation from what we know are essential skills of effective forum moderation. For example, I encouraged students to reflect carefully *before* our discussion on the questions they were to facilitate. I urged them to anticipate lines of response to their questions and consider ways to draw them out or redirect them. I also asked students to put the questions in context—by replaying, for example, a specific scene or exchange in the film that would help focus the discussion on concrete civic concerns instead of abstractions or free-floating emotional generalizations. I also gave each of the discussion leaders permission to *get personal* and to encourage us to consider a question from the vantage point of our own community experiences.

In an effort to deepen students' reflection and analysis, I asked each facilitator to write a detailed response to his or her discussion question. I added my responses to the comments on the way a moderator would respond to a forum participant, asking only questions that kept the students' thought processes on track, and then combed together all of the written exchanges into a document that contributed to the public work of the seminar and became part of its textual memory.

In the second major seminar project, held during the last two weeks of the seminar, we organized and conducted six deliberative study circle sessions on the topic "Who Is College For?" Our deliberations, based on a draft of an issue book we tested for the National Forum on Higher Education for the Public Good, addressed the forum's worries over fading support for higher education at a time when open access to colleges has never been more critical for career fulfillment and success and when the future of our national economy depends on high levels of educational attainment and performance.

The question "Who is college for?" was of immediate and particular interest to the students in the Civic America seminar. Many of them, along with their friends, siblings, and parents, had felt the financial pressures of skyrocketing tuition. Most of them held part-time jobs to cushion increasing costs of going to school. All of them had direct experience with larger class sizes at the university. Virtually all had vivid firsthand stories about perceived unfairness in college admission practices and decisions. Because they were seniors, an ancillary question—*what* is college for?—weighed equally heavily on them.

The study circles were a good opportunity, then, for my students to connect the ideas we had wrestled with in the seminar—egalitarianism, the social contract, self-reliance, among others—to reflections on their experience at a public university and their fears, hopes, and uncertainties about the future.

After one meeting drafting ground rules and plotting out the organizational contours of the study circles, we broke down into three moderator teams, each responsible for guiding deliberations on one of the three approaches to the question, who is college for?

Supporters of Approach One ("Those Willing To Work For It") believe that any student who wants to can and should attend college, regardless of their lot in life. They may need to take a longer, more difficult path, but their hard work and motivation will pay off in the end.

Supporters of Approach Two ("The Most Academically Gifted") believe that given our limited resources the best investment for the country is in those students most likely to advance society and maintain America's competitive edge in the global marketplace.

Supporters of Approach Three ("Everyone") believe that a college education doesn't merely serve individuals; it benefits everyone by strengthening society. Educated people are more engaged citizens and contribute more to society.

After the study circles, I asked each student to draft responses to a series of by-now familiar types of questions. For example: In what ways does the issue "Who Is College For?" affect you personally? What are the costs or consequences associated with each approach? Looking back on the deliberations, what are the conflicts in this issue that we still have to "work through"? Where can you detect any shared sense of direction or common ground, if any, for future action?

I also gave the study circle participants permission to reflect personally on the following questions: How has your own thinking about this issue changed? What do we still need to talk about? Why is that so difficult to talk about? How can you use what we learned in our study circle?

Once again, I combined the written responses into a document that would serve, I hope, as a lasting contribution to the narrative life of the Civic America seminar.[3]

Afterthoughts

The practices of civic culture and some of the public policy issues raised in the Civic America seminar found even more traction in conversations simultaneously taking place in my department and across the university. That same semester our provost launched a series of intense and searching discussions about rethinking liberal arts education at the university.

Meanwhile, my department formed a task force charged with reexamining the general-education writing sequence. Its report took several positions relevant to the discussions we were having in the Civic America seminar over "the one and the many." The taskforce clearly favored *pluribus* over *unum* in its vision of a socially engaged writing curriculum. It strongly recommended, for example, that the required writing course emphasize readings and diverse cultural content that honored historically disenfranchised voices and heightened students' awareness of America's changing and diverse populations and our country's problematic history of adapting to cultural differences. One of the "Guiding Assumptions" the task force proposed to shape our thinking about a new writing course, for example, stated:

> **Respond to Changing and Diverse Populations.** It is imperative that a writing program be attentive and responsive to diverse populations. Academic discourse and standard written English have excluded a multiplicity of voices alive in the American discourse for centuries, and American academia now faces the challenge of addressing unprecedented global migration. In addition to addressing linguistic diversity in our students, we must also recognize the power and potential of historically excluded discourses of race, ethnicity, class, gender, sexuality and disability.

I was under the strong influence of the core question still percolating in the Civic America seminar: Should we reconcile our many separate, communal, ethnic, and group identities with a shared identity we hold in common as Americans? If so, how? After I viewed *Farmingville*, Isaacs's warning about dismembering the body politic was no theoretical abstraction to me. Perhaps, as Robert Frost admitted about his own habit of contrariness, it was the devil in me. In any case, I drafted a sharply worded memo to my colleagues and friends on the task force, in which I sought to counter their *pluribus* with a strong dose of *unum*.

In a fervor to honor historically disenfranchised voices, we don't want to exclude cultural practices and rhetorical processes essential to making democracy work: for example, the power of public deliberation, or the rhetorical practices that diverse groups use to make hard choices together, gain clout and presence, achieve compromise, promote better understanding across lines of race, ethnicity, class, etc. Civic and public literacies, it seems to me, are far more challenging imperatives to respond to changing and diverse populations than merely opening up the canon in a required writing class and putting Frantz Fanon and Paulo Freire on our reading lists.

I had just finished my third season of purposeful deliberative learning, and I shared with the task force what I had learned: the communities—rhetorical and real—where our students live their lives, and many of the actual rhetorical situations in which they find themselves as public writers, call on them to search for common ground, act through compromise, make decisions among imperfect and incomplete choices, and search for ways to achieve and maintain social cohesion and harmony amid the acrid smoke of group differences that hung over divided communities, such as Farmingville.

ARRIVING AT THE SENIOR CAPSTONE

One advantage of using deliberative practices and active learning techniques is that the impact of subject matter often ripples outside the classroom and beyond the usual tidy brackets of the semester calendar. That was certainly the case for Sarah W., one of the members of the Civic America seminar. After the semester was over, she asked whether I would direct her senior capstone requirement. Sarah wasn't particularly excited over the prospect of conducting a research project and writing a senior paper. She lit up, however, when I suggested, "Why don't you do a full-blown public forum on the study circle topic 'Who Is College For?' in our Civic America seminar last semester?"

Sarah hit the ground running. All I did was help connect her to the right campus and community networks and meet with her regularly to help keep her on track. She did everything: media liaisoning, letter writing, scheduling, preparation of study guides and summary overhead transparencies, refreshments menu. Sarah was very nervous about moderating the forum, so I invited several colleagues and students to a practice forum at which Sarah diligently walked us through the choices, guided the conversation, and initiated reflection and next steps at the end.

"This event," Sarah wrote in a press release, "will give participants a rare opportunity to discuss the issue and work toward a common solution. It is not going to be a debate. Rather, it will be a chance to converse about an important issue that touches all of us, work toward understanding all viewpoints, and suggest some solutions." She was right. On April 12, 2005, Sarah held a small but successful deliberative campus forum on "Who Is College For?"

Afterward, Sarah submitted a bulging portfolio that chronicled her experience with the deliberative forum. The portfolio included several drafts of her evolving forum timelines, research and preparation materials, publicity kit (press releases, issue maps, posters), summary forum notes, participant evaluations, pre- and postforum questionnaires, and moderator materials (welcoming statement, transparencies, and so on). She also included a detailed reflection on her learning experiences. Here are some excerpts:

> Embarking on the Capstone Project was one of the most challenging assignments I have ever experienced. . . . I went into this project blind, but I have come out feeling confident that if ever asked to do something like this again in my life, I will be able to use the skills I learned over this semester. . . . I was able to take something I had learned in the Civic America seminar, and dive into it. Rather than simply participate in a forum and learn about the process, I was able to make the process available to the entire campus. The deliberative process is something that has become almost foreign to our society. People want to debate issues, not discuss them. Living in a democracy, it is so important that citizens are educated about their options when it comes to deciding

where they stand on issues. . . . I was able to be involved in educating the attendees on not only the topic . . . but also on the deliberative process in general. The participants walked in with one or two opinions, and left having learned to both form new opinions and to change their existing opinions. More importantly, they were able to listen to the opinions of others and witness democracy at work. . . . This was an experience that I will look back on as being something that helped me to break out of my norm and learn new skills, while also impacting my community. I am really proud of my project, and I will always value the lessons I learned through this experience.

SOME POSTCARDS HOME

I've come through these four seasons of deliberative learning with many more lessons, insights, and future challenges than I have the space to recount here. I briefly note the most important among them in the following paragraphs.

One of the things I most admire about the NIF-style of public deliberation and its adaptability to the humanities classroom is the way it respects and elevates personal experience in the calculus of public problem solving. Whenever I have the privilege of moderating a public forum or when I participate in a forum like Sarah's organized by students, I am always amazed at how powerful personal stories can be and how essential they are to public creation. Asking participants how a particular issue impacts them personally or what personal experiences have shaped their perspectives on an issue . . . these are absolutely crucial foundations for deliberation. The reciprocity between what people care about deeply and passionately and the hard work of hammering out the political will it takes to get people acting together is the greatest asset and the most daunting challenge of deliberative learning. In skillfully moderated forums, the power of personal stories—of people using their lived experience as a primary way of engaging social or political issues—is often a more fertile source of

conviction and persuasion than formal modes or skills of rhetorical train-
ing and debate or perfectly framed choices.

The same thing happens in a good personal essay. While experimenting
with these seasons of deliberative pedagogy, I also edited an international
journal of literary nonfiction—*Fourth Genre: Explorations in Nonfiction*—
that kept me in touch with good writing and the extraordinary vitality of
contemporary narrative and storytelling. Reading literally thousands of
essays submitted to the journal during that period reminded me daily that
a writer's unique voice and the palpable sense of his or her own presence
in a piece of writing are essential hallmarks of the contemporary essay. It's
interesting to me that NIF-style public forums are another discursive arena
where story, voice, and personal presence matter. In this sense, *narrative*
connected my work as a literary editor and my experiments in public conversation and deliberation in the undergraduate classroom.

When I set out on my first experiment with deliberative pedagogy for the
general-education writing course, I was much concerned about my students'
anemic civic consciousness. Like many Americans, I thought it derived from
their cynicism, apathy, indifference over conventional politics, or perhaps
a sense of powerlessness at being left out of the political equation. Accord-
ingly, in the course I posed such questions as these: Why have we withdrawn
from public association? Why have so many Americans, especially young
people, lost faith in our common life?

Given the experience of doing public work alongside this generation
through my seasons of deliberative learning and through the influence
of my colleagues at Kettering, I'm asking different questions now. For
example, how can I deepen my students' connections to the community
through the kinds of experiences that move them from an awareness of
issues into pragmatic problem-solving strategies? What forms of civic
engagements best fit my students' *personal* motivations to get involved—
especially their anger, their hope, and the realistic expectations they bring
to the work of pursuing systemic social change? Does the university's lofty
rhetoric of public service and being a good institutional citizen mask different realities that students experience in the local community—and,

indeed, on their home campuses and *especially* in my classes? And what traditions in the life of our civic culture can best sustain students' political engagement?

By helping students learn to become better interpreters of their own lives, society, and culture, my home disciplines of rhetoric and American studies—indeed, the humanities at large—can become durable and enduring resources for democracy. With their traditions of rigorous inquiry, analysis, conversation, critical reflection linked to action, and humane questioning of the status quo, the humanities are indispensable to social and cultural renewal. The humanities' quest to find truth and knowledge, as English professor Maria Farland has observed in *Higher Education Exchange* (2003), often originates in problems or challenges that should rightly be considered "public business," especially when that knowledge yields moral insight and ethical clarity or purpose into such pressing issues as mapping the human genome, preserving the natural environment, cloning controversies, reigning in youth violence, balancing individual rights and social responsibilities in the wake of 9/11, and resolving racial tensions in our communities and schools—all legitimate terrain of humanistic inquiry and insight. In short, humanists can serve the public interest by sharing their deep understanding of the roots of public problems in ways that speak to everyday experience.

To fulfill that legacy, the humanities professoriate must do a better job of closing the gap between the world of ideas and the theoretical reflexes that animate faculty culture, on the one hand, and our students' preference for concrete applications of knowledge and for active methods of learning, on the other. We need to find new and more effective ways of aligning pedagogical techniques and practices so they better address the disconnect between action and ideas that, for better or worse, characterizes the current generation of undergraduates' predominant learning style and their practices of citizenship. Such pedagogical techniques and practices include the use of active and interactive teaching and learning practices, especially the deliberative pedagogy I experimented with, where the learning ethos of the classroom—syllabus construction and management, assignments, assessment, heuristics, architecture, everything—is modeled after a public forum, and my role as teacher becomes that of a moderator and my students become agents and participants in the productive public work of the course. We also need to better integrate into the curriculum active research opportunities for undergraduates—as in Sarah's capstone—instead of using the undergraduate classroom as a site where we download our research expertise. Students need to be viewed as active producers of knowledge and agents of democracy and not primarily as passive consumers of information. Above all, we have to attend to those features and flaws of the campus culture and its disciplinary arrangements that are detrimental to civic involvement—for example, the degree to which uncontested skepticism is valued and rewarded, the absence of idealism, or the disconnect between the university's professed "mission" and its actual relationship and behavior toward the surrounding community. The same call to urgency, consequence, responsiveness, and relevance that John Dewey issued to the discipline of philosophy one hundred years ago applies even more so today to American studies, rhetoric, and the liberal arts generally. "Better it is for philosophy to err in active participation in the living struggles and issues of its own times," Dewey insisted, "than to maintain an immune monastic impeccability without relevancy and bearing in the generating of ideas of its contemporary present."

Four years ago, my first experiment with the "engaged classroom" was a reaction to an ache I felt to connect my scholarship in American studies and my teaching of writing to public issues outside of the academy. I invoked the voices of America's civic conscience—Tocqueville, Whitman, Jane Addams, Martin Luther King Jr., Robert Coles—in an effort to engage students in direct community service. I am still listening to those voices, and I continue to ask students to draw inspiration from them as well. As I have developed new ways of being in the classroom through upper division courses, seminars, and capstone projects inspired by deliberative democracy, and as I continue to enter new seasons of reclaiming the public mission of the university, I also have to pay attention to the changing voices, challenges, and learning styles of students and not hold them hostage to the political instincts of my generation, the boomer juggernaut.

The civic engagement and public work movement in the academy has allowed me to reimagine my role in the classroom and the working relationships I have with students, colleagues, and community partners. It has given me opportunities to combine the teaching of academic and public skills. It has challenged me to rethink the purposes and practices of academic scholarship in the humanities. Above all, it has renewed my hope that universities can play a dynamic role in fulfilling Jefferson's legacy and educating citizens to perform the difficult, necessary, and rewarding work demanded by a strong democracy.

NOTES

1. My colleague Laura Julier and I published a comprehensive curriculum development resource guide on this work, including a framing essay, detailed syllabi, student reflections, community partner perspectives, a portfolio of community-writing projects, and a resource bibliography. *Writing in the Public Interest: Service Learning and the Writing Classroom* is available for free download at http://www.servicelearning.org/filemanager/download/8536 _cooper-julier.pdf.

2. Fretz and I explore that collaboration in detail in our article "The Service Learning Writing Project: Re-Writing the Humanities Through Service Learning and Public Work." *Reflections* 5.1–2 (2006): 133–152.

3. That document was posted on the National Issues Forum Web site on January 19, 2005, as part of a news feature on "Deliberative Study Circles Become Part of a University Course," http://www.nifi.org/news/news_detail .aspx?itemID=2845&catID=2871.

REFERENCES

Horton, Myles. 1990. *The Long Haul: An Autobiography.* New York: Doubleday.
Isaacs, Harold R. 1975. *The Idols of the Tribe: Group Identity and Political Change.* New York: Harper and Row.

Mathews, David, and Noëlle McAfee. 2000. *Making Choices Together: The Power of Public Deliberation.* Dayton, OH: Kettering Foundation.

Veninga, James F., and Noëlle McAfee, eds. 1997. *Standing with the Public: The Humanities and Democratic Practice.* Dayton, OH: Kettering Foundation Press.

Yankelovich, Daniel. 1991. *Coming to Public Judgment: Making Democracy Work in a Complex World.* Syracuse: Syracuse University Press.

CAN CIVIC ENGAGEMENT RESCUE

THE HUMANITIES? (2013)

THE RELATIONSHIP BETWEEN THE CIVIC ENGAGEMENT MOVEMENT
and the contemporary humanities reminds me of a Nora Ephron movie
like *Sleepless in Seattle* or *You've Got Mail*. Typically, the movie begins with
two single, upwardly mobile middle-age characters who face a growing void
in their otherwise successful lives. Serendipity steers them to each other.
Circumstance or plain dumb luck often intrudes and keeps them apart.
The plot becomes a study of their romantic, often heroic, and sometimes
comic journey to find each other. Just before the movie fades to the credits,
they finally meet and either walk away together hand in hand, followed by
a golden retriever, or drive off in a Volvo.

The admittedly kitschy cinematic analogy may not be as far-fetched as it
seems when assessing the renewed commitment on the part of colleges and
universities to become more responsible institutional citizens and the struggle within the humanities to shake a two-decade-long identity crisis. In fact,
the story of two people seeking to complete each other through a longed-for
relationship fits the thrust of my argument perfectly: the civic engagement
movement needs the humanities, and the humanities need civic engagement. They belong to each other. But circumstances, professional pressures,
career demands, economic exigencies, and institutional inertia, among

other frustrations, stand in their way. I am not equipped to predict the outcome of this courtship, nor do I propose to become a matchmaker. I would like to explore, however, some of the subplots and backstories that make the relationship between civic engagement and the humanities a portrait in missed opportunities, hopeful reconciliations, and, who knows, maybe even consummation.

Those backstories, for the most part, involve complex ambivalences, issues of disciplinary self-esteem, status rivalries, and politically charged perceptions that hamper the contemporary humanities from meaningful participation in democratic renewal. At the same time, those ambivalences and perceptions, I hope to show, hint at just how important the humanities can be to cultivating the essential arts of citizenship and democracy.

I should note that common theoretical, political, social, and critical alignments are shared by many, if not most, humanities fields today. Given this sharing of orientations, I often blur lines between the cultural disciplines and address the "humanities" collectively. In particular, I focus on a brand of cultural criticism and theory—generally referred to by the deceptively generic label "cultural studies"—that cuts across and through traditional departments as well as new academic subfields like gender studies, global studies, border studies, and queer studies. With its emphasis on poststructural theory, cultural production, and radical social critique, cultural studies as a critical project capitalizes on what Stuart Hall calls "the enormously productive metaphor of hegemony" (1992, 279) that has dominated scholarship and criticism for the past twenty years. This fixation on social space as a predatory arena along with the general "cultural turn," as some put it (Sterns 2004), have made the contemporary humanities, in effect, a cross-disciplinary project.

THE HUMANITIES UNDER SIEGE

Have core humanities disciplines and subdisciplines gathered under the umbrella of "cultural studies" earned a legitimate place at the institutional table where civic engagement and social responsibility are subjects of so much spirited conversation? The answer is a reluctant no. And a qualified yes.

Ever since the late 1980s the humanities have been perceived, as Frank Rhodes, former president of Cornell University, observed, as devoted "to areas of high abstraction . . . while the larger issues of the world and humankind's place in it elude them" (Fiske 1988, B12). The widespread perception of the humanities' irrelevance to the public interest was set in motion by a tsunami of highly critical and politically charged reports, beginning with a scathing 1988 National Endowment for the Humanities white paper that blasted literary studies and theory, in particular, for preferring mind-numbing mental aerobics over fundamental questions of human purpose and moral meaning. The NEH broadside was accompanied by a volley of widely read and reviewed books whose apocalyptic titles alone speak to the siege mentality weathered by academic humanists during the late 1980s and the 1990s: *The Closing of the American Mind, Killing the Spirit, The Last Intellectuals, Literature Lost, Bonfire of the Humanities*, to name just a few. Meanwhile, American college students started voting with their feet. While undergraduates stampeded into business majors, the number of degrees awarded in the humanities began to plummet. In the mid-1970s, for every student majoring in English, for example, five of her peers were pursuing degrees in business management. By 1994, that ratio sank to one out of twenty. In a bruising 1989 NEH report (*50 Hours: A Core Curriculum for College Students*), then-chair Lynne Cheney warned: "You have students going to college who don't know what the humanities are and who may never find out." A few years later, Christopher Lasch, addressing fellow academics generally and zeroing in on the humanities professoriate in particular, scolded the "new [academic] elite," as he calls them in *The Revolt of the Elites and the Betrayal of Democracy*, for living "in a little world of their own, far removed from the everyday concerns of ordinary men and women" and speaking an incomprehensible jargon that completely subverts any "attempt to communicate with a broader audience, either as teachers or as writers" (1995, 176–178).

It comes as no surprise, then, that the humanities haven't played much of an active or, indeed, welcomed role in the national dialogue about the public roles of colleges and universities begun in earnest in the mid-1990s when "the engaged campus" and "institutional citizenship" became buzz phrases in the lexicon of higher education. Humanists are only sparsely represented, for example, in one of the most ambitious national endeavors to recover the public voice of higher learning in America. The Kellogg Forum on Higher Education for the Public Good, headquartered at the University of Michigan, sponsored four "Leadership Dialogues" in 2002 aimed at bringing together 150 prominent faculty and academic leaders committed to the academy's central role in nurturing education for liberty, democracy, and citizenship. The roster of participants reads like a who's who of university- and foundation-based civic engagement heavyweights. While that roster includes a small number of academically trained humanists who have risen to positions of leadership in academic administration, very few practicing humanities faculty have taken part in the dialogues. The ratio, for example, of humanists to social scientists is roughly one to seventeen. The numbers themselves may mean very little. But in light of the visionary moral language that energizes the Forum's mission, one has to question the missing-in-action status of the humanities and arts professoriate. The Forum architects speak of a "new covenant" between higher education and society, a sacred trust that permeates the history, the culture, the values as well as the research, teaching, and outreach practices of the academy. "Only if colleges and universities become clearer about their shared roles in service to American society," the Forum leaders write, "can they hope to maintain integrity and focus in a changing world" (Kellogg Forum 2002, 4). "Covenant," "culture," "values," "integrity," "heritage" . . . this is the turf of the cultural disciplines, the venue of their best teaching practices, their finest contributions to intellectual and public culture, and their most enduring scholarship. Yet the relative silence of humanities faculty, artists, and writers in the Kellogg Forums strikes me, paradoxically and painfully, as deafening. It points to a deep irony and a growing rift in the disciplinary culture that comprises the contemporary civic engagement movement.

This may not be such bad news at all. The awakening of social and natural science disciplines to their obligations and roles in what Ernest Boyer viewed as "the urgent new realities both within the university and beyond" (1997, 3) is cause for celebration and hope. Engaging those new realities is a healthy sign of ethical vitality as scientists (hard and soft) join their social science colleagues to examine the civic and democratic purposes of curricula, the potential of a more socially responsive and publicly intelligible scholarship, and the value of forming collaborative partnerships and conducting community-based teaching and research at their colleges and universities.

There seems to me nonetheless an inescapable paradox in the disciplinary culture that comprises and drives the agenda of the current civic engagement movement: namely, a moral language rooted in the rhetorical traditions of the humanities has been co-opted by social science at a time when the critical language of the contemporary humanities disciplines—literary studies is an obvious example—has adopted a decidedly social science inflection. Contemporary humanists, it would seem, have gladly surrendered a moral discourse shaped by twentieth-century liberalism to social scientists eager to renew their civic mission and recover their roles, first articulated by social progressives like John Dewey and Jane Addams in the 1920s, as advocates of the public good. At the same time, the humanities, once dedicated to the weighty proposition that students must think deeply about the moral and ethical issues of their own lives in order to become more enlightened and active citizens, have assumed the guise as well as the critical discourse of the social and political sciences through a preoccupation with such things as theories of social control, power, commodification, and identity politics. This inversion of roles has also made the object and aim of postmodern scholarship the mirror opposite of public scholarship. The public scholar asks, "How can the practices, methods, and conventions of my disciplinary scholarship yield knowledge that contributes to public problem solving and public creation?" The strategy of postmodernism, on the other hand, is to wrench us from what one critic calls the "charted and organized familiarity of the totalized world," "to generate rather than to purge pity and terror; to disintegrate, to atomize rather than to create a community" (Spanos 1992, 81).

A PERFECT CALM

Three forces or "fronts" are at work in the contemporary humanities that have simultaneously lined up to form a "perfect calm," marooning academic insight and critical intellect in a doldrums worlds apart from the agitations of democratic culture and the felt public sphere. In addition to a migration into the social sciences discussed above, those forces also include the triumph of high theory and a widespread and uncritical skepticism over civic culture as a broken project of the Enlightenment, another fracture in the aging, flawed bulwark of liberal humanism.

It is no profound insight to point out that high theory has supplanted affective praxis—the felt impacts of moral commitment on our actual practices of living and learning together—as the gold standard of political relevance in the contemporary humanities. When invited to speak at a Modern Language Association (MLA) Presidential Forum on scholarship and commitment, celebrated French sociologist Pierre Bourdieu offered the audience little by way of exalting the possibilities of engaged teaching and scholarship as important cultural work in the public interest. In fact, he urged higher levels of detachment from the gritty spadework of community activism, preferring instead the intellectual project of greater "critical reflexivity" as "the absolute prerequisite of any political action by intellectuals." He exhorted literary scholars to "engage in a permanent critique of all the abuses of power and authority that are committed in the name of intellectual authority" (2000, 41). Unfortunately, what Bourdieu offered as a prerequisite has become instead a substitute for public work as cultural studies scholars "interrogate" power and politics at ever higher altitudes of stratospheric abstraction and specialization. As Maria Farland has argued, "Rather than reexamining . . . disciplinary or professional affiliations to consider in what sense their work might engage questions and concerns that are public in nature, [academic professionals] have continued in the mode of specialization. . . . [I]ntellectuals remain largely disconnected from the very public which captivates them, insulated within the specialized languages and frameworks of their disciplinary knowledge" (1996, 56). For the contemporary literature classroom, one upshot is that the lived and affective impact of moral questions that might otherwise bear directly on such important matters as the dynamics of social class and the history of gender oppression get sacrificed to the clinical purity of theory and locked into a spiral of "complex relationship[s] between power . . . and exploitation," as Stuart Hall explains, "that Marxism as a theoretical project put on [our] agenda" (279).

Let me give a brief, ground-level illustration of what I mean. I recently took part in an external department review at another university. I sat in on some writing and literature classes. In one Introductory Lit section, students were immersed in a very sophisticated skein of ideas about fiction and theories of social control, about characters and the social construction of identities, and about the power dynamics of social class that were playing out in plotlines. I made a careful review of the syllabus (it was elegant) and assignments (they were thoughtful and articulate). But I also came away surprised, even a little astonished, that while students were parsing important ideas about racial, class, or gender oppression they were never invited or challenged by their professor to become intellectually, publicly, or socially engaged in those issues as they are lived out and suffered through in their own lives and local community.

Widespread skepticism throughout the humanities over foundational constructions like "civil society" or the "public good" comes at a time of deep moral ache among an American public for shared democratic truths. In a speech to the National Civic League's 100th National Conference, Daniel Yankelovich reported, well before the galvanizing events of 9/11, that American public opinion continues to reflect a widespread desire "to reconcile new social mores with American core values," including "a sense of community, neighborliness, hope, [and] optimism" (15). That sentiment was confirmed by several national surveys. They showed that the fraying of social integuments worried a majority of Americans who are eager to conciliate individual and group differences in the interest of dispelling what many perceive as a malaise that had settled over the public sphere. In one survey, 80 percent of respondents agreed that more emphasis should be put on community-building even if it meant compromising the pursuit of self-interest and individualism Americans have always cherished (Putnam 2000, 25).

Whether these public sentiments and concerns are credible or perhaps exaggerated is not at issue here. What concerns me is the stark disconnect between a public perception of civic malaise and the life and mind of the contemporary humanities. Trained in the rigorous critical skepticism of postmodern theories of power and social predation, for example, many cultural studies academics downplay reports of social or moral decline and fall as "declensionist narratives" that tend to obscure hegemonic practices lurking in the shadows of social and rhetorical fictions like the "breakdown of community" or the "decline of civic virtue." While average Americans aspire to strengthen community bonds, academic humanists have taken a sharp turn into a critique of *difference* and the ubiquitous struggle for power they perceive as the engine of human history. Asked in an interview to explain who struggles against whom, Michel Foucault replied with a degree of absolutism unusual among postmodern social theoreticians that "it's all against all. We all fight each other. And there is always within each of us something that fights something else" (115).

This fascination with the will to power as the moral pulse of the individual as well as the key to the genetic code of the body politic has not driven a scholarship, as one might otherwise expect, that would make academic postmoderns very good partners in the civic engagement movement. I am thinking of a public scholarship that meets a threshold laid down by land-grant historian Scott Peters: "how a scholar's work of constructing and communicating knowledge might contribute to community-building, to public problem solving, to public creation, and to the process of coming to public judgment on what ought to be done . . . to address important public issues and problems" (32). Liberation from constraining notions of "public," "common knowledge," and "shared truths" comes at a cost tallied by Richard Rorty, who called into question the hard inward turn of humanities scholarship and postmodernism's "spectatorial approach" to the public arena. "To step into the intellectual world which [postmodernists] inhabit," Rorty warns, "is to move out of a world in which citizens of a democracy can join forces to resist sadism and selfishness into a Gothic world in which democratic politics has become a farce" (95–96).

Rorty organizes his brutal critique of contemporary humanities scholarship around two related points. First, citing Fredric Jameson's canonical *Postmodernism, or The Cultural Logic of Late Capitalism* as an example, Rorty complains that, like the lion's share of scholarship in new hybrid fields like cultural studies spawned by celebrity intellectuals like Foucault and Jameson, *Postmodernism* "operates on a level of abstraction too high to encourage any particular political initiative" (Rorty 1998, 78). Second, while ostensibly concerned with important matters of political relevance like discrimination and oppression of minorities, the split between "spectatorship and agency," Rorty observes, renders "futile [any] attempts to philosophize one's way into political relevance. . . . Disengagement from practice produces theoretical hallucinations" (95). Never before has the critical rhetoric of the humanities been more politically inflected and ideologically supercharged. Meanwhile, never before has its intellectual world been more devoid of commitment to the commonweal, to civic activism, and to democracy as social praxis. Call it what you will—deep irony, paradox, a split between spectatorship and agency, hypocrisy, or identity crisis—the predicament of the humanities is obvious and inescapable. New culture critics can brilliantly deconstruct politics and power out of just about every text and every "artifact" of "cultural production." Meanwhile, they have very little to communicate to the larger public. They form a professoriate, as Alan Wolfe puts it simply, "that has forgotten its public obligations" (1989, 38).

RECOVERING MORAL PRAXIS

One way to reawaken the public purposes of the contemporary humanities is to reframe our teaching and scholarship as ethical practices that supplement, maybe even complement, cultural studies' critique of the politics of liberalism. I understand "ethical practice" as bound up in a pragmatic question: "How am I obligated?" The humanities disciplines, in my view, have neglected that question of moral praxis for the past couple of decades in favor of a brand of high theory more concerned with matters of power, authority, identity, and the limits of individual agency. There is a real difference, however, between radical theories of social transformation, class liberation, identity politics, and cultural production currently much in fashion in today's critical marketplace and the hard labor of democracy. That neglect of application and inattention to praxis—the bulwarks of ethical pedagogy and democratic change—is what prompts Rorty to complain about the arid material cranked out by an unself-critical and self-referential theory industry out of touch with human needs and interests.

Besides, the ideological and political agitation and the proletarian sympathies of so much academic cultural analysis are empty posturings without an activist component. This is why some humanities faculty were drawn early on to the alternatives we found in community-based teaching practices, experiential education, and the service-learning movement in the 1990s. There we met peers, senior colleagues, and mentors (in my case the Reverend John Duley, Dwight Giles, and, later, Robert Coles)—many of whom were tempered and tested by the civil rights and experiential learning movements of the 1960s (Stanton, Giles, and Cruz 1999)—with calluses on their hands and solid track records of public work in communities and neighborhoods outside the privileged, safe havens of their campus seminars.

Our students, to be sure, can benefit greatly from the political perspectives and critical insights introduced by contemporary cultural studies. Students need to know, for example, how to see through glib ideologies that cloak the trappings of abusive power and the maintenance of the political status quo. The problem, however, is that students might be overwhelmed by the ubiquitous metaphor of hegemony and led to the unfortunate conclusion that powerlessness is either inevitable or, worse, virtuous or that individual efficacy and agency are nothing more than socially constructed ideas used to enforce a discredited ideology. For me, the most important question for a socially engaged humanities curriculum is not *how* to recognize or even reclaim historically excluded groups and discourses but *what* enables diverse voices, once reclaimed, to find legitimate courses of public action that are consistent with what is valuable to the community as a whole—and not to shirk the language of consensus-building out of fealty to postmodernism's dislike of foundations and its insistence that narratives of wholeness are insidious cartoons of privilege and hegemony. This calls on us to shift the ethical center of gravity in our teaching and scholarship from "The Other" to *one another.*

REAWAKENING THE HUMANITIES

I do sense an awakening, maybe even a genuine soul-searching, in the academy and especially among humanists spurred by our loss of public purpose and relevance and the recognition that the vast majority of hyper-specialized humanities scholarship is completely unintelligible to a literate public. Concerted efforts are under way to shore up the declining cultural capital of the humanities. Nationally, for example, the consortium Imagining America is leading the way with exciting programs of renewal aimed at arts and humanities teaching, scholarship, and performance as cultural work in the public interest. Julie Ellison, founding president of Imagining America, acknowledges that there are important differences among today's humanities professoriate in our subfields and areas of specialization, in cultural agendas and professional status, and in the diverse communities and locations where we conduct our work. "But there is also startling agreement on what content is interesting," she reminds us, and "what aesthetic and thematic strands are most promising, what complexity is worth capturing. This, it seems to me, is the basis for 'educated hope' about public scholarship" (15).

At its 2004 national convention, the outgoing president of the Modern Language Association—the poster child for out-of-touch academics—organized several well-attended forums on the future of the humanities. Much frank discussion took place around the contemporary humanities' neglect of public purpose and responsibility and loss of credibility and respect in the eyes of the public. Other national organizations have devoted similar energies to repositioning the humanities into closer contact with problems and issues that confront the public today, including a book on the place of the humanities in democratic life published by the Kettering Foundation, an Association of American Universities report on reinvigorating the humanities, and a series of national leadership dialogues convened by the American Council of Learned Societies, the latter two groups not particularly known for their civic activism and agitation for public engagement.

SHUTTER TO THINK

I close here with a brief companion profile as a case study of engaged scholarship and creative activity. My purpose is to explore what these lofty national reports and heady recommendations might look and feel like on the ground. While based on my own unique experience and modest results, the broader challenges I face as a humanities scholar/teacher may nonetheless be familiar to my colleagues across the cultural disciplines, irrespective of their institutional settings: namely, the challenges of balancing, coordinating, and integrating a self-satisfying research agenda, successful peer sanction, an active teaching life, creativity, and a strong commitment to public purpose.

In my case, this balancing act has been made more urgent recently by an irresistible urge to renew a long-standing interest in photography, both as a practicing photo essayist in my spare time and as a scholar of public culture with a serious side interest in the documentary arts. How could I legitimately reposition documentary photography—something I had pursued as an avocation for forty years—into an academic vocation consistent with my appointment, something that would pass rigorous peer review while satisfying the demands of research, teaching, creative activity, and service to my university and community?

Since I could not "compete" with established photographers in my college's Studio Art Department or photojournalism colleagues in the School of Journalism, the key in my case has been to repurpose photography into a sufficiently specialized and integrated topic of investigation and a vehicle of engaged scholarship. After much research, soul-searching, and churn, I finally zeroed in on a practice of citizen empowerment and deliberative decision-making called "PhotoVoice." Used for several years internationally as a way of bringing grassroots communities and neighborhoods into the public policymaking arena, PhotoVoice puts cameras into the hands of ordinary citizens, often groups at the social margins with no experience in photography and little, if any, influence in the public sphere. After simple instruction in camera use and picture taking techniques, citizen-photographers take pictures that reflect their unique perspectives and vantage points on issues facing their communities. With the help of trained facilitators, PhotoVoice participants come together and use their photographs as prompts for discussion, reflection, and problem solving. They always exhibit their best photographs in public venues in order to engage local leaders in insightful conversations about their photographs and what light they shed on matters of community concern.

One of the first things I did was set up actual PhotoVoice projects through partnerships with local schools, neighborhood associations, and community centers. I also adapted PhotoVoice techniques to active learning practices in my classes. Fortunately, I was able to arrange a course assignment in a new Residential College in the Arts and Humanities at my university that stresses connections between student civic engagement and creativity activity. In one case, my students in a photo essay workshop designed and facilitated a PhotoVoice experience for a small group of visiting dignitaries from the West African country of Mali, including everything from an orientation workshop and guided reflection sessions to a public exhibit at the end. Another project brought together dorm students from the residential college and residents living in nearby neighborhoods to explore, through photographs, persistent myths and misperceptions about campus/community tensions. As a result of my involvement in and coordination of these PhotoVoice projects, I came to view documentary photography as an important democratic art form, a wonderful medium for storytelling, and a powerful teaching and learning tool. As an experienced journal editor, I took on an assignment as photo essay editor for a journal of literary nonfiction looking to beef up its photography section. I also accepted an invitation from an out-of-state colleague to contribute a chapter on narrative photography to a book she was editing on creative writing as social action. I received, in addition, two grants to shoot, process, draft, and design for exhibit three original photo essays of my own, two of which were published as chapbooks through a long-standing partnership I enjoy with Michigan Campus Compact.

PhotoVoice has become, in effect, a legitimate slipstream for my engaged cultural work and creative interests. It enables me to enhance my involvement with communities and publics. At the same time it is a dynamic active learning resource for classroom use. Participatory photography energizes my research agenda by refocusing (so to speak) my scholarship onto visual narrative and public documentary arts. It gives me a platform for publication and connects me to a network of like-minded colleagues and new community partners. In the bargain, it scratches my creative itch as a practicing photographer.

These criteria and impacts have been sufficient for modestly successful annual peer review. More important in my case, they are also a continuing necessity for a life.

REFERENCES

Bourdieu, Pierre. 2000. "For a Scholarship with Commitment." *Profession 2000.* New York: Modern Language Association: 40–45.

Boyer, Ernest. 1997. *Scholarship Reconsidered: Priorities of the Professoriate.* San Francisco: Jossey-Bass.

Ellison, Julie. 2008. "The Humanities and the Public Soul." *Antipode* 40.3 (June): 463–471.

Farland, Maria. 1996. "Academic Professionalism and the New Public Mindedness." *Higher Education Exchange 1996*: 51–57.

Fisk, Edward B. 1988. *New York Times*, October 5: B12.

Foucault, Michel. 1980. *Power/Knowledge: Selected Interviews and Other Writings, 1972–1977.* Ed. C. Gordon. Brighton: Harvester Press.

Hall, Stuart. 1992. "Cultural Studies and Its Theoretical Legacies." *Cultural Studies.* Ed. Lawrence Grossberg, Cary Nelson, and Paula Treichler. New York: Routledge: 272–294.

Kellogg Forum on Higher Education for the Public Good: Mission, Goals, Strategies, and Intended Impact. 2002. In *Leadership Dialogues Series 2002 Participant Binder.* Ann Arbor, MI: Kellogg Forum on Higher Education for the Public Good.

Lasch, Christopher. 1995. *The Revolt of the Elites and the Betrayal of Democracy.* New York: Norton.

Peters, Scott. 1996. "The Civic Mission Question in Land Grant Education." *Higher Education Exchange:* 25–37.

Putnam, Robert. 2000. *Bowling Alone: The Collapse and Revival of American Community.* New York: Simon and Schuster.

Rorty, Richard. 1998. *Achieving Our Country.* Cambridge: Harvard University Press.

Spanos, William. 1992. "From *The Detective and the Boundary: Some Notes on the Postmodern Literary Imagination." Postmodernism: A Reader.* Ed. Patricia Waugh. New York: Edward Arnold: 78–86.

Stanton, Tim, Dwight Giles, and Nadinne Cruz. 1999. *Service-Learning: A Movement's Pioneers Reflect on Its Origins, Practice, and Future.* San Francisco: Jossey-Bass.

Sterns, Peter N. 2004. "Teaching Culture." *Liberal Education* 90.3: 6–15.

Wolfe, Alan. 1989. *Whose Keeper? Social Science and Moral Obligation.* Berkeley: University of California Press.

Yankelovich, Daniel. 1994. "Three Destructive Trends: Can They Be Reversed?" National Civic League's 100th National Conference, Philadelphia, PA. November 11.

AFTERWORD: SPEAKING AND WORKING IN CRITICALLY HOPEFUL TERMS

SCOTT J. PETERS AND TIMOTHY K. EATMAN

In the final essay in this book, David Cooper tells a tragic story about scholars in the humanities who have detached and "marooned" themselves from the public sphere. Many readers will likely take issue with the role he assigns in this story to poststructuralist (and other) theories in the contemporary humanities. But most will share his central concern. There are forces at work within and beyond the academy that serve to separate academic life and work from civic life and work—not only in the humanities, but in every discipline and field.

Importantly, Cooper's tragic narrative of a marooning detachment in the humanities is accompanied by and held in tension with a hopeful counternarrative of civic engagement. We see this in the stories he tells about his pursuit of *learning in the plural*. This counternarrative is now emerging as a powerful (though as of yet still marginal) force in higher education. It is being written, performed, and lived out through the intellectual and public work of scholars, scientists, and artists, inside and outside the academy. Contributors to this counternarrative are developing and deploying new concepts, language, and arguments. They are proposing a long-term reconstruction and reorientation of the humanities that taps the social potential of poststructuralist and other theories by integrating them with practices that aim to make "direct and central contribution[s] to cultural problem-solving and to human development" (Newfield 2008, 145). They are also establishing new networks, journals, associations, and consortia, including one that we serve as codirectors of—Imagining America: Artists and Scholars in Public Life.

Founded in 1999, Imagining America (IA) is a national consortium of over ninety colleges, universities, and community-based cultural and arts organizations (Goettel and Haft 2012). It was born out of efforts to affirm and strengthen the significance of the cultural disciplines in both academic and civic life. Its members and participants seek to advance knowledge and facilitate learning through publicly engaged scholarship that draws on humanities, arts, and design. They—and we, as codirectors—are devoted to the work of catalyzing change in campus practices, structures, and policies that will enable publicly engaged artists and scholars to thrive, and to contribute to civic action and revitalization.

When IA was founded, much of the public engagement infrastructure in higher education was operating out of newly created centers for service learning, community-based learning, and community partnerships. Such centers offered the possibility of aligning academic work with institutional rhetoric about higher education's public purposes and mission. While values of reciprocity, mutual benefit, democracy, and the public good were often affirmed in such rhetoric, they were not always enacted in policies and practices. Centers for service learning were often established in ways that were (and still are) disconnected from academic departments and units. Despite calls for "two-way" engagement and a growing critique of one-way forms of service and outreach, scant attention was being paid to an intellectually generative power that was being fostered through partnerships between university-affiliated scholars and their nonacademic peers. And humanities, arts, and design fields were either underrepresented or absent altogether in institutional and national conversations about higher education's public engagement mission.

In an important essay, "The Humanities and the Public Soul," Julie Ellison offers a useful perspective on this absence, along with ideas for what might be done about it. "In the humanities and in many areas of the arts," she notes, "collaborative work of any kind is rare, and there is a weak tradition of partnerships by faculty, graduate students, and undergraduates with community and public partners, either individuals or organizations" (Ellison 2008, 463). Further, Ellison writes, the public engagement tradition that is relatively strong in the humanities positions scholars as oppositional social critics. Centered on the work of unmasking power and deconstructing and analyzing texts and discourse, the "public" role of the social critic has often—ironically—been practiced in the humanities in detached ways that reinforce a disconnection between scholars and their external publics.

For Ellison, a professor of American culture, English, and art and design at the University of Michigan who served as IA's founding director, the solution to this problem is not to abandon the academic work of critique and analysis. Rather, it's to look for ways to embed it in affirmative expressions of hopeful and constructive work that is not only scholarly but also *public,* in a face-to-face relational sense. Such expressions constitute a new tradition of public scholarship in the humanities. Public scholarship, Ellison (2008, 466) writes,

> is based on the conviction that it is possible for artists and humanists to make original, smart, and beautiful work that matters to particular communities and to higher education. Public scholarship provides a field for experiment, in which introspection and invention can be carried out sociably and publicly, yielding new relationships, new knowledge, and tangible public goods. The challenge for public scholars is to connect the difficulties of plausible hope with the emerging economies of cultural work.

Hope is a key word for publicly engaged forms of scholarship in the humanities. Public scholars exhibit what Ellison refers to as an "explicit hopefulness." Such a hopefulness must be "plausible," as she put it in the above passage. And it has to be tough and mature. It also needs to be critical, like the kind of hope that Paulo Freire (1992, 8) describes in this passage from his book *Pedagogy of Hope*:

> I do not understand human existence, and the struggle needed to improve it, apart from hope and dream. Hope is an ontological need. Hopelessness is but hope that has lost its bearings, and become a distortion of that ontological need. When it becomes a program, hopelessness paralyzes us, immobilizes us. We succumb to fatalism, and then it becomes impossible to muster the strength we absolutely need for a fierce struggle that will re-create the world. I am hopeful, not out of mere stubbornness, but out of an existential, concrete imperative. I do not mean that, because I am hopeful, I attribute to this hope of mine the power to transform reality all by itself, so that I set out for the fray without taking account of concrete, material data, declaring, "My hope is enough!" No, my hope is necessary, but it is not enough. Alone, it does not win. But without it, my struggle will be weak and wobbly. We need critical hope the way a fish needs unpolluted water.

The embrace and practice of a critical hopefulness in the humanities has profound implications. "Speaking in hopeful terms, for those habituated to critique," Ellison (2008, 465) argues, "puts us in a changed relationship to our cultural past and present." It can also put academics in a changed relationship with both their students and external publics, by inviting and encouraging scholars' participation in imaginative projects that aim to build up as well as deconstruct, to support as well as oppose, and to organize and participate in as well as inform and study public action and creativity.

It's not easy for academic humanists to speak and work in critically hopeful terms, to constructively, productively, and imaginatively connect and integrate hope and critique, and to do so off their campuses with diverse publics. Such work runs against the grain of academic culture. And despite some progress over the past few decades, it's still poorly understood, and it's not recognized and rewarded as much as it should be in tenure and promotion processes.

Given these challenges and problems, what can and should those of us who wish to advance public scholarship and engagement in the humanities and other fields do?

We devote the remainder of this afterword to a brief sketch of a three-part answer to this question. While the work of public scholarship is by definition collaborative, involving people within and beyond the academy, we focus our attention on those who are employed by or who are studying at colleges and universities. We do so because much of the change we need to make involves the culture and politics of the academy (of course, change is needed elsewhere, too). Those of us who work and study in higher education must become leaders and change agents in our own institutions.

RECLAIM AND RECONSTRUCT A DEMOCRATIC, CIVIC PROFESSIONALISM

The first part of our answer centers on the fundamental issue of professional identity. This is not an esoteric issue. The way we in the academy understand our identities as professionals influences and shapes the way we understand who we are and what we do, and why it matters.

Public scholarship in the humanities can be viewed as an expression of a particular kind of professionalism in the academy (and elsewhere) that has deep historical roots. Such a professionalism includes not only the competent and ethical performance of technical skills but also the purposive pursuit of democratic values, interests, and ends. It situates professionals *in* rather than apart from or above civic life, as citizens (in an inclusive, nonlegal sense) who perform work that has cultural and political as well as technical value and significance. Scholars have begun to name and theorize this kind of professionalism in their research and writing as "democratic professionalism" (Dzur 2008) and "civic professionalism" (Bender 1993; Sullivan 2005; Boyte and Fretz 2010).

Because the humanities have long been viewed as having not only personal but also civic dimensions and value, civic professionalism in the humanities shouldn't be a stretch to imagine. In theory, the humanities can do such things as cultivate critical intelligence, heighten historical consciousness, foster an awareness of moral complexity, foster healthy skepticism, enlarge our sympathies for and understanding of others, and enhance our capacity to evaluate and judge our interests, ideals, and ends (Peterson 1987).

To move beyond theory, we need to operationalize the civic dimensions and value of the humanities in our practices as scholars. For such work to be supported and sustained as legitimate, we will have to reclaim and reconstruct a democratic, civic professionalism in the institutional routines and policies of the academy, including graduate education, professional development, and tenure and promotion processes. The crucial step, of course, is not simply to call for this to be done, but to actually do it. But how?

Happily, this is not a hypothetical question. Efforts to reclaim and reconstruct civic professionalism in the humanities and other fields in the academy are already well under way (Ellison and Eatman 2008; Jay 2012; Haft 2012). We can learn a great deal from those who have already set about the task—including David Cooper. His book is rich with lessons from the field.

TEACH AND PRACTICE A DIFFERENT KIND OF POLITICS

The second part of our answer centers on another fundamental issue: politics. In our view, a reconstructed civic professionalism needs to be expressed through the practice of a different kind of politics than the kinds that tend to be dominant in the humanities, in higher education, and in our broader society. With respect to the humanities, Ien Ang (2006, 185) has offered a sharp critique of the kind of politics that's practiced by some humanities scholars who locate themselves in cultural studies:

It is fair to say that as an intellectual practice confined almost exclusively within the academy, cultural studies is by and large seriously disengaged from the messy realities of social and political struggles of the day. Too often what is presented as radical or transgressive is no more than discursive posturing, performed as a kind of what Slavoj Zizek calls "cultural studies chic." Connor argues that cultural studies people should abandon the "grandiose delusion" that their work is actually a way of doing politics: "I have come to think that the work of politics is vastly necessary and for the most part tedious; the study of culture is endlessly fascinating and pretty much gratuitous." Baetens makes a similar observation: "Assuming you can combine both, i.e. doing politics when doing your job inside the academy, is an insult to all those who are really doing politics in the field."

Ang's critique—and Žižek's and Baetens's, whom he cites—is useful. (So, too, is the critique Cooper offers in this book.) But critiques aren't enough. And they aren't always helpful, particularly if they suggest that scholars should abandon the idea that their work *can* be a way of doing politics. And particularly if they lead people to believe that *all* cultural studies scholars embrace and practice the same kind of "discursive posturing" politics. This simply isn't so. Imagining America wouldn't exist if there weren't scholars who were not only yearning for but already practicing a kind of politics different from the kind that Žižek calls "cultural studies chic." Such scholars have shifted how they understand not only what their work is, but also where it's practiced.

The work of public scholars isn't limited to criticism. And it isn't confined within the academy. It's engaged in, rather than disengaged from, the messy realities of social and political struggles. And at its best it's not tedious. It's just as endlessly fascinating and gratifying as the study of culture. That's partly true because at its best public scholarship *includes* the study of culture. It draws on and integrates sophisticated conceptual tools from poststructuralist and other theories in publicly oriented and situated practices.

For us, public scholarship at its best is practiced as a kind a democratic populist politics that Harry Boyte refers to as "everyday politics"

(Boyte 2004). Everyday politics of this sort reflects a view of politics as an activity people engage in when they work together across lines of difference to advance their interests and values. The practice of this kind of politics includes naming and framing common problems; expressing and examining values, interests, and desired ends and goals; considering what can and should be done to address common problems and pursue interests and ends; building and exercising power; and acting together in ways that involve reconciliation and negotiation over different and often conflicting values, worldviews, interests, and ends. It's less about protest than it is about getting things done. Less about mobilizing exclusive interest groups than it is about organizing diverse and inclusive publics. Less about winning causes than it is about building power and developing leadership that can be exercised to solve problems and advance self-, common, and public interests.

In short, to deal with the challenges that stand in the way of advancing and strengthening public scholarship in the humanities, we need to teach and practice a democratic populist politics that has a deep, full participation ethos. Such a politics is not instrumental or transactional but richly relational and transformative. While it includes "reasoned" discourse and deliberation, it also includes storytelling and the expression of emotion. And it's centered on creative, productive public work that produces products with cultural as well as technical value.

The kind of politics we're talking about here requires skilled relational organizing (Payne 1995/2007; Chambers 2003; Avila 2010). Organizing that isn't only or even mainly about solving problems, but rather about strengthening people's civic agency, talents, and imagination in ways that build and sustain public relationships. Organizing that honors and enacts in the humanities and arts a role that C. Wright Mills (1959, 191–192) once assigned to the social sciences: the "educational and political role of social science in a democracy is to help cultivate and sustain publics and individuals that are able to develop, to live with, and to act upon adequate definitions of personal and social realities."

SHARPEN AND SUSTAIN A CRITICAL DISCOURSE

Finally, closely interwoven with the above parts of our answer we need to set about the task of expanding and sharpening a critical discourse about higher education's public mission and work, in and for a democracy (Peters 2010). Such a discourse should focus on the critical issue of professional identity—of who academics are, what they do, and how and why it matters—as well as the issue of politics. We have good reasons to disagree with each other about these issues. And given the contingencies and complexities of context, we need ways to attend to them that are not dogmatic or ideological.

The critical discourse we need should involve the posing and exploration of key philosophical and empirical questions. For example: What meanings do we invest in our identities as *professional* educators, artists, and scholars who happen to be employed by academic institutions? Specifically, how do our identities inform and shape our understanding of what our work is, including our roles and contributions in society, beyond the classrooms, offices, libraries, and laboratories of our campuses? And how—if at all—do our identities as professionals connect with our identities as agents and citizens (in an inclusive, nonlegal sense) in a democracy?

The critical discourse we need should include attention to problems *in* democracy, such as inequity, poverty, and climate change. But it should also include attention to problems *of* democracy, such as the lack of democratic publics, citizens that have been sidelined from the work of politics, and the power, effects, and behavior of special interest money and groups. Among the many problems of democracy, of special need of attention for academic professionals and institutions is the problem of the role and function of experts and science, both of which can have either technocratic or democratic aims and implications (Fischer 2000; Jewett 2012).

Perhaps most important for us, the critical discourse we need must not be limited to arguments about ideas and theory, expressed in academic jargon. It must also be expressed in everyday language, and grounded everyday life. And it must be fueled and informed by stories about our experiences and work.

We need to encourage more critically reflective discourse, writing, research, and storytelling from those who are engaged in the work of public scholarship, and the work of reclaiming and reconstructing a civic, democratic professionalism in the academy. We have our own vehicle for this at Imagining America: a multimedia, open-source journal called *Public* (public.imaginingamerica.org) that actively solicits and publishes submissions about the public engagement work of scholars in humanities and design fields as well as artists.

While writing and publishing are key parts of the critical discourse we need, it's likely that the most important part is social. We need a critical discourse that offers opportunities for face-to-face interaction between and among people from all walks of life, inside and outside the academy. We need skilled organizers and facilitators who know how to use it to "cultivate and sustain publics and individuals that are able to develop, to live with, and to act upon adequate definitions of personal and social realities." And we need—all of us—to learn how to engage in it in ways that activate a critical hopefulness, and that facilitate a productive and imaginative *learning in the plural*.

REFERENCES

Ang, I. 2006. "From Cultural Studies to Cultural Research: Engaged Scholarship in the Twenty-first Century." *Cultural Studies Review* 12.2: 183–197.

Avila, M. 2010. "Community Organizing Practices in Academia: A Model, and Stories of Partnerships." *Journal of Higher Education Outreach and Engagement* 14.2: 37–63.

Bender, T. 1993. *Intellect and Public Life*. Baltimore: Johns Hopkins University Press.

Boyte, H. C. 2004. *Everyday Politics: Reconnecting Citizens and Public Life*. Philadelphia: University of Pennsylvania Press.

Boyte, H. C., and E. Fretz. 2010. "Civic Professionalism." *Journal of Higher Education Outreach and Engagement* 14.2: 67–90.

Chambers, E. T. 2003. *Roots for Radicals: Organizing for Power, Action, and Justice.* New York: Continuum.

Dzur, A. W. 2008. *Democratic Professionalism: Citizen Participation and the Reconstruction of Professional Ethics, Identity, and Practice.* University Park: Pennsylvania State University Press.

Ellison, J. 2008. "The Humanities and the Public Soul." In "Practicing Public Scholarship: Experiences and Possibilities beyond the Academy." Ed. Kathryn Mitchell. Special issue of *Antipode: A Radical Journal of Geography* 40.3: 345–497.

Ellison, J., and T. J. Eatman. 2008. *Scholarship in Public: Knowledge Creation and Tenure Policy in the Engaged University.* Ann Arbor, MI: Imagining America.

Fischer, F. 2000. *Citizens, Experts, and the Environment: The Politics of Local Knowledge.* Durham, NC: Duke University Press.

Freire, P. 1992. *Pedagogy of Hope: Reliving Pedagogy of the Oppressed.* New York: Continuum.

Goettel, R., and J. Haft. 2012. "Imagining America—Engaged Scholarship for the Arts, Humanities, and Design." *Handbook of Engaged Scholarship: Contemporary Landscapes, Future Directions.* Ed. H. E. Fitzgerald, C. Burack, and S. D. Seifer. East Lansing: Michigan State University Press.

Haft, J. 2012. Publicly Engaged Scholarship in the Humanities, Arts, and Design. Published online by Animating Democracy. animatingdemocracy.org/resource/publicly-engaged-scholarship-in-humanities-arts-design#.UQWc1qVKmzc.

Jay, G. 2012. "The Engaged Humanities: Principles and Practices for Public Scholarship and Teaching." *Journal of Community Engagement and Scholarship* 3.1: 51–63.

Jewett, A. 2012. *Science, Democracy and the American University: From the Civil War to the Cold War.* Cambridge: Cambridge University Press.

Mills, C. W. 1959/2000. *The Sociological Imagination.* New York: Oxford University Press.

Newfield, C. 2008. *Unmaking the Public University: The Forty-Year Assault on the Middle Class.* Cambridge: Harvard University Press.

Payne, C. M. 1995/2007. *I've Got the Light of Freedom: The Organizing Tradition and the Mississippi Freedom Struggle.* Berkeley: University of California Press.

Peters, S. J. 2010. *Democracy and Higher Education: Traditions and Stories of Civic Engagement.* East Lansing: Michigan State University Press.

Peterson, M. D. 1987. *The Humanities and the American Promise: Report of the Colloquium on the Humanities and the American People.* Austin: Texas Committee for the Humanities.

Sullivan, W. M. 2005. *Work and Integrity: The Crisis and Promise of Professionalism in America.* San Francisco: Jossey-Bass.

ACKNOWLEDGMENTS

The writing in this collection spans twenty years. Over that time I have accumulated a sizable ledger of debts to hundreds of students, colleagues, and community partners, far too many to acknowledge here by name. I hope that a sincere and collective thank-you for their generosity, hard work, patience, and infectious learning spirit will suffice.

I extend special thanks to those colleagues who have stood by me and contributed time, wisdom, and their shared faith in public work with me across two decades of "learning in the plural": Frank Fear, Eric Fretz, Dwight Giles, David Stowe, Lynnette Overby, Jeff Grabill, Janet Swenson, John Duley, Jeffrey Howard, Parker Palmer, Harry Boyte, Robert Coles, Patti Stock, Pennie Foster-Fishman, Richard Bawden, James McClintock, Sally McClintock, Harry Reese, Sandra Reese, Douglas Noverr, Gary Hoppenstand, Nancy DeJoy, James Porter, John Kinch, Arthur Versluis, Ken Waltzer, Terry Link, Ann Austin, John Beck, Pat Enos, Rachelle Woodbury, Jessica Rivait, Jan Hartough, Wynne Wright, Elaine Brown, Kenneth Fields, Marjorie Ford, Ann Watters, James Karagon, Nicholas Holton, Marylee Davis, Bill Hart-Davidson, Laura Julier, and Ralph Menendez, and to all my colleagues who participated in the Service Learning Writing Project (especially Lynn Scott, John Dowell, and Fred Barton).

I am grateful too for the leadership of Stephen Esquith, founding dean of the Residential College in the Arts and Humanities, and Patrick McConeghy, Acting Dean of the College of Arts and Letters at Michigan State University (2004–2006), for his support of the Public Humanities Collaborative I founded and directed from 2005 to 2010. And to all my colleagues at the PHC (in particular, Howard Bossen, James Detjen, Len Fleck, Jim Lawton, Marsha MacDowell, and Paul Thompson), especially my dear friend Eileen Roraback, Associate Director, graduate assistants Jennifer Nichols, Ildi Olasz, and Aimee Knight, and PHC Faculty Fellows (Kirk Domer, Salah Hassan, Xiaoshi Li, Ann Mongoven, Juan Javier Pescador, Rob Roznowski, Leonora Smith, Hsiao-Ping Wang), I extend my gratitude for helping establish an active center for public humanities on campus.

Operating foundations and professional nonprofit organizations are often "colleges" for faculty like me who work camouflaged, whether by design or necessity, on the edges and in the seams of their home institution. They are crucial places where we learn, grow, stretch intellectually, test out new ideas, and bond with like-minded colleagues. For me those vital learning places include, first and foremost, the Charles Kettering Foundation (Derek Barker, David Brown, John Dedrick, David Mathews, Maxine Thomas, and Deborah Witte), especially my Kettering work group on Deliberative Democracy and Higher Education (Christina Alfaro, Allison Crawford, Harris Dienstfrey, Michael D'Innocenzo, Joni Doherty, Larkin Dudley, Maria Farland, Laura Grattan, Katy Harriger, Lee Ingham, Jill McMillian, Dennis Roberts, and Doug Walters); the John Fetzer Institute; the Kellogg Forum on Higher Education for the Public Good (John Burkhardt and Tony Chambers); Michigan Campus Compact (Allison Treppa, Rene Miller Zientek, and former executive directors Lisa McGettigan Chambers, Jenni Holsman, and Amy Smitter); the Midwest Campus Compact Collaboration; Campus Compact (Elizabeth Hollander); the Invisible College (John Wallace, Edward Zlotkowski, Nan Skelton, Nancy Kari, Ira Harkavy, and Richard Cone); the Learn and Serve America Exchange Program supported by the Corporation for National Service and the National Youth Leadership Council (Linda Jacobson, Project Director); and especially Imagining America (Julie Ellison, Jan Cohen-Cruz, Scott Peters, Juliet Feibel, and Timothy Eatman).

My learning community at Michigan State University extends far beyond my home department and college, and includes MSU's Center for Service Learning and Civic Engagement (Karen Casey and Mary Edens); the Residential College in the Arts and Humanities (Vincent Delgado, Candace Keller, Carolyn Loeb, David Sheridan, Anita Skeen, Mark Sullivan, and J. Estrella Torrez); the Office of University Outreach and Engagement (Hiram Fitzgerald, Burton Bargerstock, Diane Doberneck, and Patricia Farrell); the Bailey Scholars Program; the Morrill Scholars Program (Michael Koppisch and Tess Tavormina); the MSU Museum (Kurt Dewhurst and Julie Avery); the Writing Center (Patti Stock); and, not the least, the Center for Community and Economic Development (Rex LaMore, John Melcher, and Faron Supanich-Goldner).

Finally, I thank Gabe Dotto and Michigan State University Press for giving me the rare opportunity at the endgame of a career to sort through, sift, and reflect over my teaching, writing, and learning life during these past two decades.

The essays and articles in *Learning in the Plural* first appeared in the following publications:

"Believing in Difference: The Ethics of Civic Literacy." *Educational Forum* 57.2 (1993): 168–177.

"Moral Literacy." *Journal of Value Inquiry* 28 (1994): 297–312.

"Reading, Writing, and Reflection." *Academic Service-Learning: A Pedagogy of Action and Reflection.* Ed. Robert A. Rhoads and Jeffery Howard. New Directions for Teaching and Learning Sourcebook Series No. 73. Gen. ed. Robert Menges. San Francisco: Jossey-Bass, 1998: 47–56. Also appeared as "Reading, Writing, and Reflection." *The Campus Compact Toolkit.* Providence, RI: The National Campus Compact, 1999.

"The Changing Seasons of Liberal Learning." *Midwest Quarterly* 37.2 (1996): 119–137. Also appeared as "The Changing Seasons of Liberal Learning." *Literacy Matters: Reading and Writing in the Second Wave of Multiculturalism.* Ed. Lillian Bridwell-Bowles. Upper Saddle River, NJ: Prentice-Hall, 1998: 309–322.

"Academic Professionalism and the Betrayal of the Land-Grant Tradition." *American Behavioral Scientist* 42.5 (1999): 770–779.

"Bus Rides and Forks in the Road: The Making of a Public Scholar." *Higher Education Exchange* (2002): 24–36. Reprinted in *Campus Compact Reader: Service-Learning and Civic Engagement* (Spring 2002): 1–3; 14–18. Also appeared in different form as "The Roads Mistaken: Merging the Pathways of Profession, Community, and the Inner Life." *Trying the Ties That Bind.* Kalamazoo, MI: John Fetzer Institute, 2000: 137–157.

"Education for Democracy: A Conversation in Two Keys." *Higher Education Exchange* (2004): 30–43. Reprinted in the *Campus Compact Reader* (Fall 2004): http://www.compact.org/reader/. Also appeared as "The New Student Politics: A Boomer's Commentary." *Journal of Public Affairs* 7.1 (2004): 87–101.

"Is Civic Discourse Still Alive?" *Museums and Social Issues: A Journal of Reflective Discourse* 2.2 (2007): 157–163. Reprinted in *The Friday Letter* (Kettering Foundation). Ed. Robert Daly. May 25, 2007: 41–49.

"Four Seasons of Deliberative Learning: From General Education to the Senior Capstone." *Deliberation and the Work of Higher Education: Innovations for the Classroom, the Campus, and the Community.* Ed. Harris Denisfrey, John R. Dedrick, and Laura Grattan. Dayton, OH: Charles F. Kettering Foundation, 2008: 113–143. Portions reprinted in *Kettering Foundation Reader on Civic Education.* Ed. David Brown and Derek Barker. Dayton, OH: Kettering Press, 2009.

"Can Civic Engagement Rescue the Humanities?" Chapter 17 in *Going Public: Civic and Community Engagement, the Scholarship of Practice.* Ed. Hiram Fitzgerald and Judy Primavera. East Lansing: Michigan State University Press, 2013. Also appeared in different form in *Literature Matters: Community-Based Learning and the Work of Literature.* Ed. Sue Danielson and Ann Marie Fallon. Boston: Anker Books, 2007: 1–25.